WHEN
PROPHETS
PREACH

Praise for *When Prophets Preach*

Jay Augustine's newest book, *When Prophets Preach*, makes clear the power that can come from the pulpit, as preaching—effective, inspired preaching—brings heaven's voice to the very real hurts and injustices of this world.

—The Most Rev. Michael B. Curry, Presiding Bishop
of The Episcopal Church and author of *The Power of Love*

When Prophets Preach clearly identifies the challenge of prophetic preaching that is both divinely inspired and socially determined. Using Jesus as a model for the prophetic preacher, Jay Augustine makes the case that the traditional salvific message of the gospel is not in competition with the message of social justice/prophetic preaching. Rather, he establishes the necessity for prophetic preaching in an era in American culture that is rife with injustice, inequality, and the dangerous rise of an evangelical liberalism that supports, rather than condemns, these kinds of inequities. This book is a must-read for anyone who dares enter the pulpit. It challenges all proclaimers of the gospel to be relevant in their preaching about the ways in which the real lives of people are being impacted by today's social ills and the message of hope that comes through the Christian faith.

—Bishop Teresa Jefferson-Snorton, Ecumenical Bishop
and Program Development Officer,
Christian Methodist Episcopal Church

Unpacking the alchemy of gospel proclamation and social transformation, Jay Augustine offers a field guide for aspiring prophets. A historic and biblical survey with urgent summons and a toolbox for reconciliation and repair, *When Prophets Preach* is essential reading for clergy and congregations seeking to grow their courage and translate ideals of justice into action.

—Rev. Dr. Katie Crowe, senior pastor,
Trinity Avenue Presbyterian Church

In *When Prophets Preach*, Jay Augustine makes an overwhelmingly convincing case for political witness and social-justice action in the ministry of the churches, such that if one reads it thoroughly, one is likely to suspect cowardice if the prophetic dimension finds no place in preaching and general pastoral leadersip. Hopefully, digesting the spirit of this work will lead clergy and laity alike to pray earnestly for the courage to bear witness to the truth and justice God demands of us all.

—James A. Forbes, senior minister emeritus,
The Riverside Church, New York

Jay Augustine proves again that he is an incisive and insightful practitioner of the Black prophetic tradition. *When Prophets Preach* helps the reader to clearly distinguish the difference between the liberation theology of the Black church and the dangerous ideology of white Christian nationalism. Using his bivocational voice as a legal scholar and theologian, Augustine helps us follow the path of the proclamation of the good news from a contested tradition toward reclaiming a crucial trajectory in the fight for justice, equality, and democracy. This book breathes new life into the homiletic task, activating a vital method for engaging contemporary Christians in the good fight of faith toward realizing a reconciled, restored, and redeemed Beloved Community.

—Lester A. McCorn, president, Clinton College

The Reverend Attorney Jay Augustine demonstrates once again what a great asset he is to the body of Christ. In this volume he not only gives the reader a historical sketch of the benefits of what prophetic preaching has meant to the Black church and, more importantly, to the Black community, but he also challenges the present-day preacher to reclaim their position as the Lord's instrument for liberation and empowerment through prophetic preaching and leadership. This is a must-read!

—John R. Bryant, senior bishop (ret.), African Methodist Episcopal Church

When Prophets Preach: Leadership and the Politics of the Pulpit is a cogently written, thought-provoking, troubleshooting tool for both new and seasoned clergy to advance the pastoral ministry. The author presents various viewpoints to stimulate discussion and reflection through his views and personal commentaries. Jay Augustine challenges readers to formulate their position based on prophets' unique ability to use the pulpit as a platform for healing churches, communities, and the problems impacting today's global society. *When Prophets Preach* is another giant step forward in addressing issues affecting our local and international communities and the critical role of the pulpit in orchestrating high-quality solutions for pulpit and pew as partners in spiritual, emotional, physical, social, and mental awakening processes for resolving both local and global problems.

—Bishop James Levert Davis, Presiding Prelate, Second Episcopal District, African Methodist Episcopal Church

As a preacher, I am intimately aware of the excuses, exhaustion, equivocation, rationalization, and real fear that keep a sermon from addressing injustices of the day. This book is the call to courage that will be on my desk at all times. With history, theology, and no-holds-barred present-day examples, Jay Augustine offers preachers the pep talk we need to face this moment.

—Rev. Rebecca Gillespie Messman, senior pastor,
Burke Presbyterian Church (USA)

Jay Augustine brilliantly and insightfully weds his high social-justice IQ with his considerable skills and gifts as a preacher-scholar to gift the church in general, and preachers in particular, with this timely challenge to regain our prophetic voice. The fragile democratic experiment of the American Empire continuously battling internal forces of neofascism and a world trying to rebuild in the shadows of a death-dealing pandemic beg for prophetic preaching that is a mirror, depicting the ills and injustices of the body politic, and a window, through which we can re-vision, with hope, what is possible. Caution: Read this book and be prepared for pulpit renewal, church revival, and a social and political revolution that may "turn the world upside down."

—Frederick Douglass Haynes III, senior pastor,
Friendship-West Baptist Church, and author of
*Rockin' the World with Your Words: An Essential Guide
to Developing and Delivering a Life Changing Message*

In a historical moment when personal piety without community accountability unfortunately has ascended as the popular mode of spiritual discourse, thought leader, activist, and preacher Jay Augustine has recalibrated our focus toward justice with this book. The prophetic tradition articulated in this publication is the balm our nation needs to confront the trauma of our unexamined history and to heal. This publication deserves a space on bookshelves and university curriculum across this country.

—Otis Moss III, senior pastor,
Trinity United Church of Christ,
and professor of homiletics,
McAfee School of Theology

Jay Augustine is a preacher, a pastor, a poet, and a prophet. His passion comes through on every page, and the text is both inspirational and concretely helpul—a rare combination. *When Prophets Preach* is a must-read for every preacher who longs to do justice from the pulpit.

—Mindy Makant, dean of the College of Humanities and Social Sciences, Lenoir-Rhyne University

WHEN PROPHETS PREACH

Leadership and the Politics of the Pulpit

Jonathan C. Augustine

Foreword by William J. Barber II
Afterword by William H. Willimon

FORTRESS PRESS
MINNEAPOLIS

WHEN PROPHETS PREACH
Leadership and the Politics of the Pulpit

Copyright © 2023 Fortress Press, an imprint of 1517 Media. All rights
reserved. Except for brief quotations in critical articles or reviews, no part
of this book may be reproduced in any manner without prior written
permission from the publisher. Email copyright@1517.media or write to
Permissions, Fortress Press, PO Box 1209, Minneapolis, MN 55440-1209.

All Scripture quotations, unless otherwise indicated, are from the New
Revised Standard Version Bible, copyright © 1989 National Council of the
Churches of Christ in the United States of America. Used by permission.
All rights reserved worldwide.

Scripture quotations marked (NIV) are from the Holy Bible, New
International Version®, NIV®. Copyright © 1973, 1978, 1984, 2011 by
Biblica, Inc.™ Used by permission of Zondervan. All rights reserved
worldwide. www.zondervan.com The "NIV" and "New International
Version" are trademarks registered in the United States Patent and
Trademark Office by Biblica, Inc.™

Scripture quotations marked (RSV) are from the Revised Standard
Version of the Bible, copyright © 1946, 1952, and 1971 National Council
of the Churches of Christ in the United States of America. Used by
permission. All rights reserved worldwide.

Cover image: Micah Exhorts the Israelites to Repent, Gustave Dore 1866
Cover design: Brice Hemmer

Print ISBN: 978-1-5064-7918-7
eBook ISBN: 978-1-5064-7919-4

To the living legacy of those prophetic preachers who sought to transform institutional norms of *injustice*, into societal norms of *justice*, through their activism. Although your names are too numerous to list, it is to you this book is respectfully dedicated.

CONTENTS

FOREWORD

Few voices in American life are more dangerous than those who describe themselves as prophets. Whether they claim a special word from God about the secret to your financial success or a special anointing on some politician, most people who publicly claim the label of "prophet" grossly misuse the term. And yet, at the same time, we are in desperate need of authentic prophetic preaching—the kind of public truth-telling that has shaped moral movements in US history from abolition to women's suffrage to the 20th century's struggles for labor rights, civil rights, and economic justice.

Dr. Augustine is right: we need prophetic preaching. But we need to be clear about what the prophetic vocation really is. That's why I'm grateful for this book. It makes clear that there is a rich tradition from which we can draw for prophetic witness today, and that this tradition is not an add-on to the gospel, but essential to the gospel. In short, this isn't simply a call for some to preach this tradition in some moments. It is, rather, like the Letter from a Birmingham Jail, a convincing case that prophetic preaching is normative preaching.

To preach has always meant more than oratory and words. To preach is to proclaim. It is to speak to the death of our times words that take on flesh and challenge the forces that kill. A preached word is not anything until it takes on flesh and gets to work. The living Word of God always renders a reorientation in our way of life.

"Preach the good news at all times," Saint Francis of Assisi said. "When necessary, use words."

Preaching must beget a living contradiction to the hate and meanness of the times. It is to always have a quarrel with the world's deeds of injustice. True preaching cannot rest on the page, sit in a song, or travel on a tweet alone. No, the preached Word must put on flesh and suit up for struggle. If it doesn't, it's not preaching.

Moses preached, and his preaching turned into a movement that challenged the oppression of Pharaoh.

Isaiah preached, but his words called for deeds when he asked:

> *"Is not this the kind of fasting I have chosen:*
> *to loose the chains of injustice*
> *   and untie the cords of the yoke,*
> *to set the oppressed free*
> *   and break every yoke?*
> *Is it not to share your food with the hungry*
> *   and to provide the poor wanderer with shelter—*
> *when you see the naked, to clothe them,*
> *   and not to turn away from your own flesh and blood?*
> *Then your light will break forth like the dawn."*
> * (Isaiah 58:6–8 NIV)*

Amos preached to raise a remnant that would let justice roll down like waters and righteous like a mighty stream.

Ezekiel preached to turn a valley of dry bones into an army of hope.

Sojourner Truth preached and spoke a relentless passion for liberation into the hearts of her hearers.

William Lloyd Garrison preached, and he made abolition his cause.

Fannie Lou Hamer preached, standing up for freedom and never accepting compromises.

Rabbi Abraha Joshua Heschel preached, drawing on the Torah to frame the struggle for civil rights. The confrontation between Pharaoh and Moses was not over, he declared. "Pharaoh is not ready to capitulate. The exodus began, but is far from having been completed. In fact, it was easier for the children of Israel to cross the Red Sea than for a Negro to cross certain university campuses."

Heschel declared that racism is equal to Satanism. Religion and racism cannot coexist because it violates the command not to murder. In fact, racism is condemned in the Talmud as equal to murder.[1]

Heschel put legs on his preaching and prayers when he marched across the Edmund Pettus Bridge, standing alongside black people as a colleague and challenging racism.

Martin Luther King, Jr. preached, but his words were not just soaring oratory. King preached upon the foundation of civil disobedience and called forth a movement to challenge the demons of Jim Crow. His preaching confronted racism, poverty and war, not only within the quarantine of the sanctuary, but in the streets of the nation.

Dorothy Day preached love through the pages of the *Catholic Worker* newspaper, but she also lived out revolutionary love in hospitality houses for the poor. "When lines of people began to form, saying, 'We need bread,' we could not say, 'Go, be thou filled,'" Day wrote. "If there were six small loaves and a few fishes, we had to divide them." She knew there was no way to preach the words of Jesus without following the way of Jesus.

Jesus came preaching with power and authority because his preaching laid out mission and ministry in the face of the narcissism and cruelty of tyrants in his day. His preaching was, from the start, a call to action.

In his very first sermon, in his own hometown, Jesus preached:

"The Spirit of the Lord is on me,
  because he has anointed me
  to proclaim good news to the poor.
He has sent me to proclaim freedom for the prisoners
  and recovery of sight for the blind,
to set the oppressed free,
  to proclaim the year of the Lord's favor."
    (Luke 4:18–19 NIV)

And at the end of Matthew's Gospel, in one of his last sermons, Jesus preached:

"For I was hungry and you gave me something to eat, I was
thirsty and you gave me something to drink, I was a stranger
and you invited me in, I needed clothes and you clothed me,
I was sick and you looked after me, I was in prison and you
came to visit me . . . Truly I tell you, whatever you did for one of
the least of these brothers and sisters of mine, you did for me'"
(Matthew 25:35–36, 40 NIV).

So if preaching is only words and does not lead to acts of liberation with and on behalf of the poor, the imprisoned, the sick, the oppressed, and all those made to feel accepted, then preaching is just words with no purpose, talk without action, lip service without love, the sound and the fury that signifies nothing.

"If I speak in tongues of men and angels but have not love," the apostle Paul says, "I am nothing" (1 Corinthians 13:1, 2 RSV). And love, my friends, is an action verb.

Preaching is only authentic when it is embodied by the deliver and inspires action in the hearer.

Who are the poor, the blind, the oppressed, the prisoners and unaccepted among us today?

Are they the 140 million in poverty in America alone?

The 37 million without access to healthcare?

The 4 million who can buy unleaded gas but can't get unleaded water?

Are they those facing the racism of voter suppression?

Are they the thousands trapped in a new Jim Crow, where the blacker and browner and poorer you are, the more likely you are to be in prison?

Are they the gay, the trans, the bi, the queer?

Are they the women mis-used, the children abused?

To preach is to see, to say, and to do.

It is to see the people who are crying out and the systems that are crushing them.

It is to say, "Somebody's hurting my people, and it's gone on far too long. And we won't be silent anymore."

It is to do something about it. To join with others who are doing something about.

When words are turned into deeds of liberation, that's preaching. Anything else is just talking.

When the fruit of the lips become actions dedicated to justice, that's preaching.

When our words call Jews, Muslims, Christians, Sikhs, Buddhists and even people not of faith to come together in the work of love and liberation, that's preaching.

When a call goes out that unites people across lines of race and class and creed and sexuality, that's preaching.

When the Poor People's Campaign brings Native and Asian, black, white, and brown together to work together and march together and organize together and go to jail together for a moral revolution of values, that's preaching.

When preachers at the border serve communion and offer hospitality, that's preaching.

When nuns lobby for healthcare, that's preaching.

When churches open their doors and offer sanctuary to families that are being ripped apart by ICE, that's preaching!

I pray this book will stir the Word up within you and within this land. I pray it will call everyone who reads it to take up the prophets' true mantel and preach with words and deeds the possibility of lifting from the bottom so that everyone can rise.

Bishop William J. Barber II
Advent, 2022

INTRODUCTION
The Preaching of Twenty-First-Century Prophets

> But how can they call on one in whom they have not believed? And how are they to believe in one of whom they have never heard? And how are they to hear without someone to proclaim him?
>
> —Romans 10:14

I took a leap of faith when I left a successful pastorate with a historic congregation in my hometown of New Orleans to serve an unfamiliar congregation in Durham, North Carolina. While meeting with each auxiliary, ministry, and stakeholder at St. Joseph AME Church, and as I attempted to learn from the congregation's respective groups and formulate strategies for growth, it became abundantly clear that the congregation was thirsting for "prophetic preaching."

During my initial May through early June 2019 stakeholder meetings, I was proudly reminded that as a pastor and preacher of the gospel, I am part of an institution with a storied past that is anchored in social justice. Not only is the church universal's institutional past anchored in the fight for social justice, but the concept of "speaking truth to power" is also inextricably linked to the church's present and future. Indeed, speaking out against social injustice is at least one of the two reasons the church was born. The original/first-century church was birthed to address (1) salvation in the "kingdom to come" and (2) social injustices in the "kingdom at hand." Prophetic preaching does exactly that.

A Call from the Pew to the Pulpit

Notwithstanding the church universal's proud institutional past, the church has a sincere problem in the present. Specifically, so many pastors shy away from prophetic preaching, failing to address matters of social injustice from the pulpit. As a pastor who watches and often preaches about the news, I wonder how so many preachers could *not* address social injustices. Because so many don't, there is a definitive need in the current church to (1) speak to the importance of prophetic preaching and (2) recontextualize the prophet's twenty-first-century leadership role.

What Exactly Is "Prophetic Preaching"?

Prophetic preaching is both divinely inspired and socially determined. In the seventh and eighth centuries, biblical prophets shared prophecies, or what we might call sermons, that were both revelations from God *and* responses to social situations.[1] Similarly, God reveals to the contemporary preacher the importance of addressing injustices that arise in the current social order. Stated otherwise, the social justice–oriented preacher might address issues like mass incarceration, the separation of migrant children from their families at the US/Mexico border, and environmental degradation. The language the preacher uses to invoke outrage at such situations will be determined by social circumstances.

The American church needs the prophet's voice because someone must preach that global warming—and more specifically, corporate pollution—is destroying the planet. Someone needs to preach that Christian nationalism and xenophobia are wrong, especially when Christians vilify people of other faith traditions because it becomes politically expedient, particularly in election years. Walter Brueggemann writes, "Prophetic ministry has to do not primarily with addressing specific public crises but with addressing, in season and out of season, the dominant crisis that is enduring and resilient."[2] Indeed, there is a need for twenty-first-century prophets to preach and create an alternative to the dominant culture's embrace of hyperincarceration and predatory practices that continue to plague and marginalize poor Black and brown communities. Prophetic preaching is a ministry led by divine revelation and in response to specific social circumstances that often speak in opposition to the dominant culture, much in keeping with the old expression of "speaking truth to power."

According to Marvin A. McMickle, the function of prophetic preaching is to shift a congregation's focus from what's happening to them as a local congregation to the broader concern of what's happening to them as part of society.[3] Prophetic preaching must provoke the listener to look at the macro impact of cultural norms instead of adopting a micro perspective. The church's prophetic voice is speaking truth to power in addressing matters like the crumbling infrastructure in public schools and the chauvinistic sexism of pay disparities between men and women.

Prophetic preaching is often interpreted as apocalyptic and specifically dealing with the "end times." In actuality, however, it is just the opposite. Prophetic preaching deals with the current times and is reminiscent of the biblical prophets' calls to live out God's vision for peace, justice, and equality. Laura Tubbs Tisdale describes it as the kind of preaching that can "get ministers in trouble."[4] Rather than adopting a static definition, Tubbs Tisdale contextualizes prophetic preaching by highlighting several of its hallmarks, including a concern with evils and shortcomings in the present social order while also being focused on political issues, being countercultural and challenging the status quo, offering hope of a new day to come with the promise of liberation to God's people, and providing encouragement to listeners while empowering them to work and change the social order.[5]

In Paul's clarion call for applied leadership in preaching, he asks, "How can they call on one in whom they have not believed? And how are they to believe in one of whom they have never heard? And how are they to hear without someone to proclaim him?" (Rom 10:14). The contemporary American church needs preachers—*modern-day prophets*—who are not afraid to "get in trouble" and speak truth to institutions of power by providing a voice for those who have been marginalized and pushed to the social and socioeconomic periphery as well as calling out paradigms that improperly influence American life, like the conflation of cross and country that creates the inappropriate and exclusionary cultural framework of Christian nationalism.

Prophetic preaching *is not* just about biblical texts, as in preaching from the Bible's Prophetic Books. It is instead about promulgating God's word from a liberative perspective that focuses on justice and equality within both the church and society at large and promotes human empowerment in response to social marginalization. As a reconciliation advocate and someone firmly committed to creating community instead of chaos, my response to the dominant cultural narrative of inequality in America is often rooted in preaching an ethic of racial and gender equality to provide hope and encourage the church to be engaged in the fight for equality in the "kingdom at hand," instead of simply waiting for God's glorious reign in the "kingdom to come."

In August 2020, for example, during the Covid-19 pandemic, my mainly Black congregation commemorated the fifty-seventh anniversary of the March on Washington with our majority-white sister congregation, St. Paul's Evangelical Lutheran Church. In emphasizing the importance of people coming together for a common purpose, I preached from the topic "Coming Together as One," applying Paul's egalitarian ethic of unity and equality in the body of Christ. Just as Paul rejects ethnic and gender distinctions between Jews and gentiles to emphasize unity within the church (Gal 3:23–29), I did the same. I rebuked the politicization of a calculated polarization between Blacks and whites, suburbs and cities, and Republicans and Democrats during ongoing #BlackLivesMatter protests. By focusing on *unity,* and not division, the sermon identified issues and proposed solutions instead of ignoring political occurrences.

Prophetic preaching should always invoke a divinely inspired and social justice–oriented response that provides hope for humanity, specifically rebuking any dominant norms of marginalization and oppression of any of God's children based on human-made social constructs.

So Why Don't Preachers Preach Prophetically?

To return to my May 2019 assignment to serve St. Joseph, the thirst for prophetic preaching was so prevalent because it was not present in the years immediately prior to my service. As typical with so many ministers who only address salvation in the kingdom to come, they neglect to direct the church universal's social compass in the kingdom at hand. Prophetic preaching should encourage church leaders, clergy and lay alike, to respond to social issues affecting the world through the domain of prophetic leadership.

Jesus's ministry is an exemplar of prophetic leadership, as he speaks to social justice issues. As the writer of Luke shares, Jesus begins his public ministry by professing, "The Spirit of the Lord is upon me, because he has anointed me to bring good news to the poor. He has sent me to proclaim release to the captives and recovery of sight to the blind, to let the oppressed go free, to proclaim the year of the Lord's favor" (Luke 4:18–19). Indeed, as Obery M. Hendricks Jr. notes in *The Politics of Jesus: Rediscovering the True*

Revolutionary Nature of Jesus' Teachings and How They Have Been Corrupted, Jesus's inaugural sermon announced that the reason for his anointing by God and the purpose of his worldly mission are one and the same—to proclaim radical economic, social, and political change. Stated otherwise, Jesus's ministry is prophetic because he speaks out for those who are socially marginalized due to their circumstances and the structures of certain social institutions.[6] Accordingly, the model for the preacher speaking out like a prophet—addressing salvation in the kingdom to come *and* matters of social (in)justice in the kingdom at hand—comes directly from Jesus, a prophetic preacher and leader.

Karl Barth's well-known and time-honored expression "The preacher should preach with the Bible in one hand and the newspaper in the other" advocates for prophetic preaching by metaphorically placing an emphasis on the importance of making the Bible's lessons applicable to contemporary times. In the image of Jesus, therefore, twenty-first-century prophetic preachers should live out Barth's advice by breaking the pulpit silence and speaking to matters like those of social justice, just as Jesus would if he were preaching today.

Here is the conundrum: Jesus was a prophetic preacher; Christian ministers are presumably called to be "Christlike" in ministry, yet there is a dearth of twenty-first-century prophetic preachers. Why do so few contemporary preachers address social justice issues from the pulpit? Although Jesus began his ministry, by his own account, challenging unjust systems and shaking up the status quo, many twenty-first-century preachers are more interested in status quo preservation than in change. *Why?*

The prophet's work is not easy. In some regards, the prophet's motivating force, although it may sometimes seem harsh, is sharing God's liberating love and speaking out for justice.[7] While so many twenty-first-century lectionary preachers teach (and preach) from the Bible's Prophetic Books, their Advent reliance on Isaiah and Micah "limits" them to joyfully reminding the world that Jesus was born according to messianic prophecy (see, e.g., Isa 7:10–16; Mic 5:2–5a). The contemporary prophet's work, especially in the realm of preaching, cannot be confined by the liturgical season. People need to hear from the God of liberating love and justice throughout the entire year. But how can they hear without a preacher (Rom 10:14)?

Perhaps, with piety often preempting politics, some preachers are more concerned about individual conduct than they are about communities in despair. With the rise of megachurches and so many preachers' unwillingness to say anything unpopular—even in Black church traditions, where prophetic preaching may be expected—some pastors don't want to rock the boat by disrupting "praise parties" to force disquieting reflection on social justice matters. Indeed, the message so many megachurches preach, one rooted in prosperity theology, focuses much more on material success than on the social gospel.[8] The church should never become so "heavenly holy" that the church can no longer be any earthly good. Stated otherwise, a large segment of the contemporary church is so focused on the kingdom to come that it has lost sight of social issues in the kingdom at hand. There is still a need for prophetic preaching.

Social justice begins with the liturgy of lament. However, it is impossible to jump hastily to social justice without first doing the hard work of owning and acknowledging the social *injustices* that are so prevalent in America. In other words, the dominant parties (the majority-white denominations or congregations) must confess wrongdoings, while the oppressed parties (the majority-Black denominations or congregations) must acknowledge the pain of their oppression. This might explain why so many contemporary American churches avoid lament in worship.

Further, increased congregational offerings come more so from praise parties than experiences of introspective reflection. It is therefore understandable—considering the realities of parishioners' individual spheres (e.g., child-rearing, marriage)—that some preachers refrain from prophetic preaching to avoid emotionally burdening parishioners. Before moving to the solution, however, there must be an acknowledgment of the underlying problems. To paraphrase the prophet, Can these bones live (Ezek 37)? Who will do the hard work of the prophet and speak?

Prophetic preaching cannot be limited by the liturgical calendar or contained only in the Prophetic Books of the Holy Bible. It must move the local church's focus from what is happening to the individual to what is happening to the church as a part of society. In shifting the congregational focus, the prophetic preacher should prompt the congregants to ask, "What is the role or the appropriate response of our congregation, our association, and our denomination to the events that are occurring within our society and throughout the world?"[9] Just as Paul says, "How are they to believe in one of whom they have never heard? And how are they to hear without someone to proclaim him?" (Rom 10:14). The prophet must preach! More specifically, the prophet must preach *prophetically* by interrogating the biblical text to see how it speaks in modern contexts.

Prophetic Leadership Is a Part of the Threefold Office

Prophetic preaching is a part of the prophetic leadership domain and the *munus triplex* doctrine, also called the threefold office, which explores priestly and kingly (royal) leadership too. Through the lens of prophetic leadership, the calls for prophetic preaching and the ministry of reconciliation come together. Courage is needed in prophetic leadership to address topics of social injustice and fulfill the ministry of reconciliation that Jesus left to the church (2 Cor 5:17–19).

Jesus's leadership is typically viewed through his varied roles as a prophet, priest, and king (or royal). Although the threefold office's terminology is traditionally used to describe *ecclesial* leadership, there are also three very similar interactive dimensions in *secular* leadership: direct, relational, and instrumental.[10]

Direct leadership takes charge, like a king. Relational leadership offers care and enhances others' self-worth, much like a priest. And instrumental leadership motivates others into new ways of seeing and acting, like a prophet. Although the "prophet, priest, and king" leadership model is not static and its domains will most certainly overlap, its rubric provides an effective framework to explore the need for prophetic preaching as a part of prophetic leadership.

The kingly (royal) domain categorizes leadership as building infrastructure for people and protecting them while also making decisions about the allocation of scarce resources and creating optimism during the inevitability of a crisis. A classic example of royal leadership in the secular context is the role of a chief executive when a crisis arises. The corporate CEO is expected to chart a path for the company and its directors during the inevitable crisis. At the federal level, the president is supposed to do the same while remaining composed and optimistic as the country faces an unprecedented crisis. Moreover, the governor and mayor should do the same at the state and local levels, respectively. This is the essence of direct leadership.

The priestly domain categorizes leadership in a way that creates meaning for people in an organization through story and consensus building while also helping create order. In the secular context, a priestly leader could be a nonprofit CEO who brings her team together by focusing on the significant community impact of their mission and work, instead of dwelling on the fact that the organization is underfunded. Moreover, in the ecclesial context, the pastor who visits a terminally ill parishioner in hospice, leads the inevitable celebration of life, and provides hope for a grieving family is an exemplar of a priestly leader. The priestly leader epitomizes relational leadership.

With respect to prophetic leadership, however—the lens through which this book should be viewed—a prophetic leader exposes systems that are unjust and unfair while speaking truth to power in attempting to change those systems. Inasmuch as the term *prophetic* readily invokes images of many Old Testament prophets who carry the charge of literally speaking truth to power, also consider the way in which Jesus's ministry begins—Luke describes him prophetically preaching his first social justice sermon. Jesus came to bring good news to the poor, proclaim release to the captives, and let the oppressed go free (Luke 4:18–19)! In the contemporary context, we might say Jesus came to address issues like poverty, food scarcity, and the problem of mass incarceration—issues that go beyond the anticipated perfection of the kingdom to come by dealing with the reality of imperfections in the kingdom at hand.

Although Jesus's ministry is the perfect exemplar of all three domains of ecclesial leadership, this book focuses on his *prophetic* leadership and the need for more prophetic preaching in local congregations. While instrumental leadership in the secular context is critically important in motivating others to recognize alternative views and see new possibilities and relational leadership is equally important in creating optimism in the face of circumstances that might otherwise cause despair, this book's focus speaks to the moral imperative given to members of the church to speak out against social injustices.

Where Do We Go from Here?

Prophetic preaching seeks to engage more preachers in the work of twenty-first-century prophets. In chapter 1, "When Does the Church Get Political?," I highlight the sociopolitical circumstances that led the Black church to become prophetically engaged in the politics of the civil rights movement. As the chapter overviews the internal philosophical conflict between politics and piety that has long existed—whether the church should deal only with salvation or simultaneously advocate for matters of social justice—in the same mold of Jesus taking on the secular political systems of his day, the Black church wrestled with this dilemma before ultimately leading the church universal into secular politics. Although the Black church is not monolithic, chapter 1's exploration is a road map for others, particularly those in mainline denominations that have traditionally refrained from addressing politics from the pulpit. Chapter 1 also lays a foundation for this book's recurring references to Christian nationalism, one of the things that is most polarizing in America. While it is a phenomenon that is intertwined with so many aspects of the American church's twenty-first-century existence, Christian nationalism has nothing to do with religious orthodoxy but is concentrated in a political framework centered on the power dynamics of Otherism's "us versus them." This divisiveness calls the American church's modern-day prophets to preach!

Chapter 2, "Reckoning, Reconciliation, and Repair," discusses the concept of reconciliation in America through the lens of race while simultaneously defining it in a threefold context: *salvific*, *social*, and *civil*. Insofar as salvific reconciliation deals with salvation *through Jesus*, the apostle Paul's theology of equality connects salvation to the equitable treatment of others *because of Jesus*. This is called social reconciliation. The consequence, illustrated when the church demands governmental and political reforms to protect marginalized groups, is called *civil reconciliation*. In recognizing America's current divisions, this is indeed an area from which prophets must preach!

In chapter 3, "Profiles in Prophetic Leadership," the ministry of reconciliation is highlighted in the work of both individuals and movements. The chapter focuses on the work of Dietrich Bonhoeffer and Martin Luther King Jr. while also drawing a connection between the clergy-led resistance of the twentieth-century civil rights movement and the ethical resistance of the twenty-first-century

#BlackLivesMatter (BLM) movement. Although the recent BLM movement's origins are more rooted in secular notions of justice, the two are connected in that they both responded to a social narrative of marginalization that necessitated action. In other words, just as Daniel 3's story of civil disobedience motivated King in writing "Letter from Birmingham City Jail," King's political organizing motivated many contemporary BLM protesters in countless American cities.

Chapter 4, "Social Injustices the Church Cannot Ignore," celebrates the ethic of prophetic resistance and connects public protest to immoral social matters such as failed immigration policies. While encouraging ministers to engage in civil disobedience, chapter 4 builds upon chapter 3 in maintaining that the church has a moral responsibility to speak out and lead from the prophetic domain on matters where society is adversely affected. Stated otherwise, chapter 4 argues that the church must be engaged in more than just preaching salvation in the kingdom to come. It must also prophetically address social injustices in the kingdom at hand.

Finally, in chapter 5, "The Practice of Prophetic Preaching," proven strategies for pastors are discussed, in leading from the prophetic domain, to plan local church calendars that focus on both liturgy and public life, thereby affirming church members' identities. Consider the first three months of the year, for example, if the local church does more than a perfunctory observance of Martin Luther King Jr. Day in January. Think about a culturally competent Black History Month worship celebration in February—*especially in predominately white congregations*—as well as a Women's History Month celebration in March. Inasmuch as these strategies have worked in my ministerial contexts, they will work in others too.

Conclusion

Prophetic preaching in the local congregation has the potential that formerly inactive members will become active again and many new members will join. Most importantly, however, in formulating a response to matters of social (in)justice, prophetic preaching and leading from the prophetic domain can motivate congregation members to not just take moral positions on contemporary issues but also act out in furtherance of their positions. Each week, prophetic preachers responsibly use both the Bible and the newspaper in worship and address social injustices the body of Christ simply cannot ignore.

Jonathan C. Augustine
August 28, 2022
Durham, North Carolina

WHEN DOES THE CHURCH GET POLITICAL?

> Religion operates not only on the vertical plane but
> also on the horizontal. . . . On the one hand, it seeks to
> change the souls of men, and thereby unite them with
> God; on the other hand[,] it seeks to change the envi-
> ronmental conditions of men so that the soul will have
> a chance after it is changed.
>   —Martin Luther King Jr., *Stride toward Freedom*

The combined roles of the church, as a vehicle for salvation *and* as an advocate for social justice, can be summarized by Reverend Dr. Martin Luther King Jr.'s reference in the epigraph to the Christian cross having two planes: the vertical and the horizontal. The vertical plane represents the church's salvific work in reconciling humanity to God with an eschatological focus on the kingdom to come. The cross's horizontal plane, however, represents the church's social role in reconciling human beings with one another with a justice-oriented focus on the kingdom at hand. King's clear reference was that the church has more than one purpose and more than one function. His ministry exemplified this message.

As an ordained minister, King preached about salvation in the afterlife. Moreover, as a prophetic leader who was a member of a marginalized social class, he also preached about social injustices in this life. King's ministry was not only exemplary of how piety and politics should work together in the church, but it was also revolutionary. With an eye toward reconciliation, he literally moved the church into the realm of secular political engagement.

King was born in 1929, the son of a prominent Black pastor, and aware of the Black church's political gospel of "Jesus and Jobs"— in response to the difficult economic conditions brought on by the Great Depression of the 1930s and the frequent employment discrimination Blacks faced in the years that followed—when he was growing up in the 1940s, during the Great Migration. At that time, many Protestant clergypersons were going through a transition from Fundamentalism to an emerging Liberalism, which would later have a significant impact on King's theology. Influenced by Baptist minister and civil rights leader Benjamin Mays at Morehouse College as well as some of the leading liberal theologies at Crozer Seminary and Boston University—including Walter Rauschenbusch's Social Gospel, Reinhold Niebuhr's Christian realism, and L. Harold DeWolf's (Boston) personalism—King's lived experiences and academic exposure shaped his perception of race relations and active leadership in the Black freedom struggle.[1]

As King grew to lead a prophetic ministry of social change, there were at least two areas of theological agreement he shared with prominent theologian Walter Rauschenbusch: "(1) Religion must concern itself with not only the *future* but also the *present* life, ministering not merely to the individual person but also to the person's environment. (2) The pulpit must be used not only for the effective dissemination of such a concept if social evils are to be eliminated."[2] This theology—that the church must bear witness in the realm of social justice—greatly shaped King's ministry and the church's political evolution during the civil rights movement.

In his first book, *Stride toward Freedom: The Montgomery Story*, King describes his leadership philosophy by writing, "The Christian ought always to be challenged by any protest against unfair treatment of the poor, for Christianity is itself such a protest."[3] Using the progressive politics of Protestantism and its practical application in his pulpit at Dexter Avenue Baptist Church in Montgomery, Alabama, King rose as a nascent leader in the civil rights movement as he expected the social and salvific realms of Christianity to meet in challenging unjust secular systems. Changing souls and bringing them to unification with God was one thing—an important thing. For King, however, the church's work was not limited to salvation in the kingdom to come. He also believed the church had a moral responsibility to address matters of social injustice in the kingdom at hand. King's ministry, therefore, raises this book's foundational question, especially through the realm of prophetic preaching: When does the church get political?

The question of when an ecclesial body decides to become involved in secular politics is inspired by the late Manning Marable. Using the Black church as an example, he observes the separation between faith and the political praxis of Black clergy that many Black theologians and sociologists of religion made. He points out that so much of political science research regards King as a centrist, within a broad and fractious desegregation campaign, while ignoring the historical connection between faith and politics. Marable highlights that there is a lack of research focused on the impact of the civil rights movement on the evolution of the Black church.[4]

To pick up where Marable left off, with his specific example of the Black church, this chapter's larger contextualization of the church universal shows that the church "gets political" and has gotten political—as it did during the twentieth-century civil rights movement—in response to the twenty-first-century's oppressive social conditions. No conditions have more recently necessitated prophetic political action than the ongoing policies and politics that were and continue to be with the "Make America Great Again" (#MAGA) political narrative.

Although #MAGA is widely associated with the 2016 presidential election, its regressive politics are not limited either in America's sociopolitical chronology or to a particular politician. Instead, its cultural framework embraces some of the greatest threats to American democracy, including racial and ethnic subjugation, voter suppression, and Christian nationalism.

Unfortunately, just as the church has responded well to some issues of social injustice, it has completely failed to respond to others. Anytime injustice is prevalent and the church abdicates its moral responsibility to address it, the church's ministers are preaching a truncated gospel.

Why Is There a Tension between Piety and Politics?

It might seem as though piety and politics have competing interests in the church—one is largely focused on the afterlife and the other deals with the current life. Prophetic leadership exemplifies how they should complement, rather than compete against, each other. Stated otherwise, the church's priestly work should not be in competition with its prophetic work, just as its salvific work should not be in competition with its role in social justice. In addition to being a vehicle for salvation, the church is also supposed to both serve and advocate on behalf of "the least of these" (Matt 25:40). The priest's work, preaching salvation in the kingdom to come, *is not* in competition with the prophet's work, speaking truth to power in the kingdom at hand.

The tension between pietistic theology and political activism is nothing new. Indeed, King's prophetic leadership fell into ongoing tensions within Black church communities, as illustrated by the initial resistance to his liberationist theologies during the civil rights movement. Further, in more mainline church communities today, there are still philosophical differences between the more conservative evangelical "private church" (where the focus is on saving souls in the private world of religion) and the more liberal "public church" (where Christians are compelled to go public with their social agenda). In other words, some still say that the church should not be involved in politics, while others ask how it can't *not* be involved in politics.

The word *politics*, as translated from Greek, simply means "affairs of the cities." Consequently, when the church "gets political," it addresses matters of the state that morally compel its active engagement and prophetic resistance. Indeed, the Bible is replete with examples of prophetic leaders who get political because their faith compels responses to social injustices. Amos's cries for justice in the northern kingdom of Israel are political (Amos 5:4, 24). Paul's pronouncement of gender and ethnic equality, in speaking against the patriarchal norms of his Greco-Roman world, is also political (Gal 3:28). John is political too in writing from the penal colony of Patmos to the seven churches that are being oppressed by an unjust Roman government (Rev 1:9). Consider also the three Hebrew boys: Shadrach, Meshach, and Abednego. They most certainly are political when they engage in civil disobedience by refusing to obey King Nebuchadnezzar's dictates with a willingness to accept the consequences of their actions (Dan 3).

In *The Politics of Jesus*, Obery M. Hendricks Jr. highlights that when the Hebrews escape oppression in Egypt, there is a turning point in the biblical narrative. Like a line of social demarcation, the Bible moves from individualism and individual deliverance to communalism, as an entire religious community is liberated through collective deliverance. This transition makes the exodus a *political* event, as an entire class of subjugated people moves from the grip of economic exploitation and oppression.[5] By therefore viewing the exodus as such, Moses becomes "political" when he embraces an ethic of prophetic resistance and courageously stands to tell Pharaoh that God says, "Let my people go!" (see, e.g., Exod 5:1; 9:1).

Christianity compels political engagement in responding to oppressive social conditions. Stated otherwise, when conditions necessitate, the church should never be reluctant to get political by engaging secular authorities. Any theologies that dispute the fact that Jesus's prophetic leadership spoke to social injustices refuse to acknowledge the full scope of his ministry. He spoke out against the socially oppressive conditions that subjugated him and his fellow Jewish brothers and sisters living under Rome's imperial domination (Luke 4:18–19). Part of Jesus's duality was ushering in salvation in the kingdom to come while also speaking to social injustices in the kingdom at hand. Stated otherwise, Jesus was political!

Jesus's Ministry of Salvation and Social Justice Was Inherently Political!

The unjust political systems of Jesus's day necessitated his prophetic response. In his formative years, he naturally would have been influenced by the Roman colonial occupation of Israel. Public crucifixions were commonplace as a means of intimidation, just as were public lynchings in the Jim Crow South. The trauma the people of Israel suffered during Jesus's earthly life heavily impacted the political and social realms and caused serious emotional harm to Jews. Even though Jesus was the Son of God, he was also a Jew who was oppressed by the politics of the governing Roman power structure, which diminished his human worth.

The politics of poverty, debt, and taxes also influenced the oppressive sociopolitical climate in which Jesus lived. For example, Luke's popular story about Zacchaeus, the tax collector, acknowledges how Roman authorities often engaged willing parties to defraud subservient Jews with inflated tax collections, thus keeping them impoverished and consequentially in debt (Luke 19:1–10). Further, Jesus expressly mentions debt default in Matthew while asking for *debt forgiveness* in such ways that suggest Jews were oppressed by the politics of poverty as part of their cultural existence.

In addressing the phenomenon of a subservient class of Jews being marginalized, as Jesus offered prophetic leadership in ministry, Matthew's Gospel references debt default as if it were a social reality with which everyone was familiar (18:23–35). Indeed, when the disciples ask Jesus how to pray and *what to pray for*, Jesus tells them, "Forgive us our debts" (6:12).[6] This again notes the politically oppressive governance under which Jesus lived and served in ministry.

Jesus's reference to praying for debt forgiveness, taken from his famous Sermon on the Mount (Matt 6:12), reflects his prophetic leadership, as salvation and social justice go hand in hand. In following Jesus's example, modern-day ministers must also provide prophetic leadership in response to contemporary forms of social oppression by likewise getting political.

Connecting the Present and the Past by the Need for Prophetic Preaching

Because of the ecclesial hierarchy and structure of so many churches, getting political will almost always begin with preaching—specifically, *prophetic preaching*. Prophetic preaching begins with its specific task: moving a congregation's perspective from individual matters to more social matters as they consider how they fit into the larger world picture. William H. Willimon shares it best in *Leading with the Sermon*, as he writes, "In preaching, God's people are moved, that is *led*—little by little, or sometimes violently jolted . . . Sunday by Sunday, toward new and otherwise unavailable descriptions of reality."[7] Indeed, moving people to see new things is consistent with the instrumental leadership of the prophet, in leading from the prophetic domain.

In more liberationist faith traditions, prophetic preaching does not regard social justice as separate from God's word. Instead, as with other sacred values, prophetic preaching emanates from God's word.[8] Stated otherwise, prophetic preaching should be a fundamental part of responding to social injustices by preaching with the Bible in one hand and the newspaper in the other. This practice in preaching brings the biblical text to life for contemporary believers who are wrestling with contemporary issues. For prophetic preaching to be heard, in provoking a response to social injustices, modern-day prophets will have to find the courage to stand up in the face of those who believe the church should not be involved in political affairs and preach the *full* gospel! Jesus died. But Jesus also lived. And Jesus's life included an earthly ministry that focused on social justice.

Twentieth-century Jim Crow laws were oppressive and marginalized people based on race. Both laws and social customs devalued ethnic and religious minorities and pushed them to America's social periphery. Such laws and their consequential oppressive conditions sparked King's twentieth-century prophetic leadership, as social circumstances necessitated that the church respond. Similarly, the much more recent #MAGA political narrative also marginalized racial and religious minorities while simultaneously objectifying women. The point of comparison is that just as Jim Crow laws necessitated a prophetic response, the oppressive #MAGA cultural framework does too. #MAGA birthed the responsive fusion politics of church coalitions and faith-based groups, as the church "woke up" to create a counternarrative sparked by powerful prophetic preaching.

Building on Brueggemann's conceptualizations, prophetic preaching is often countercultural in that it creates an alternative narrative to the dominant culture. Because the #MAGA cultural framework can be used to see much broader problems in America, it represents a larger political divide that includes race and class as well as a gap in values and governing priorities. Prophetic preaching seeks to create an alternative point of view.

America's Climate of Christian Nationalism Requires a Prophetic Response

Race is merely a social construct whereby an associated value is assigned.[9] It is not inherent in the human condition. By therefore emphasizing the need for prophetic preaching, I am calling out a cultural framework that is rooted in Otherism and that values certain classes of people as less than others and sets social policies pursuant to those valuations. It is not OK to create and maintain a culture that condones singling out Mexicans by categorically calling them thugs and rapists. It is not OK to vilify Muslims by collectively calling them terrorists. It is not OK to claim Haitian and African immigrants come from "shithole countries." This cultural framework is Christian nationalism, a conflation of cross and country that propagates political divisions based on race and ethnicity.

To provide a clear definition for this cultural framework, sociologists Andrew L. Whitehead and Samuel L. Perry, in *Taking America Back for God: Christian Nationalism in the United States*, contextualize Christian nationalism by providing the following definition:

> We mean "Christian nationalism" to describe an ideology that idealizes and advocates a fusion of American civic life with a particular type of Christian identity and culture. We use "Christian" here in a specific sense. We are not referring to a doctrinal orthodoxy or personal piety. (In fact, we find some Christian nationalists can be quite secular.) Rather, the explicit ideological content of Christian nationalism comprises beliefs about historical identity, cultural preeminence, and political influence.... This includes symbolic boundaries that conceptually blur and conflate religious identity (Christian, preferably Protestant) with race (white), nativity (born in the United States), citizenship (American), and political

*ideology (social and fiscal conservative). Christian national-
ism, then, provides a complex of explicit and implicit ideals,
values and myths—what we call a "cultural framework"—
through which Americans perceive and navigate their social
world.*[10]

Indeed, the #MAGA political narrative represents the horrific culmination of an ongoing division and divisiveness in America that
has become part of the cultural norm.

The conflation of cross and country undermines democracy
because, in the most exclusionary form, Christian nationalism seeks
to maintain the status quo and preserve power for "we the people."
In considering who *is* and who *is not* included in the "we," Christian nationalism is a powerful predictor of intolerance toward
immigrants, racial minorities, and non-Christians.[11] A powerful
demonstration of this dangerous cultural framework is the so-called
replacement theory as documented in a 180-page white supremacist manifesto associated with the targeted mass shooting of African
Americans on May 14, 2022, in Buffalo, New York. The theory—a
belief that Blacks and Jews are replacing whites in America's sociopolitical hierarchy—is also what undergirded the hate exemplified
by Dylann Roof, the white supremacist who horrifically assassinated
the Emanuel Nine (Pastor Clementa Pinckney and eight members of
his midweek Bible study) on June 15, 2015, at Mother Emanuel AME
Church in Charleston, South Carolina. This fear of replacement and
attempt to preserve the original racial hierarchy of America is part of
Christian nationalism's ongoing influence.

The entire message of the #MAGA political narrative, in
both the 2016 and 2020 presidential elections, was about restoring
power to a demographic that feels it has lost power to immigrants,
minorities, and Jews. With a philosophy of American exceptionalism that goes hand in hand with manifest destiny, a belief that
America is destined by God to expand its dominion across North

America, the two political ideologies connect to undergird the cultural framework of Christian nationalism whereby any group that attempts to make changes to the established American order becomes a target for violent attack.

The type of Christian nationalism that has been used to motivate occurrences like the January 6, 2021, insurrection against the US government is a call for the prophet to preach. The attack was a blatant attempt to violently overthrow the government rather than respecting the rule of law or *civilly* disobeying it. The insurrectionists sought to supplant it. Multiple insurrectionists were photographed with paraphernalia saying either "In God We Trust: Stop the Steal" or "Jesus is My Savior, Trump is My President." Several others carried life-size replicas of Jesus's cross. Such public expressions reveal an inherent conflation of cross and country undergirding a sense of American exceptionalism that regards America as God's chosen nation, on par with the nation of Israel. In considering Whitehead and Perry's definition, however, Christian nationalism *is not* about church orthodoxy. It's a cultural and political framework that seeks to preserve a power often associated with America's original white Anglo-Saxon hierarchy.

Prophetic Preaching Is Responsive to Social Circumstances

There is a huge difference between the Bible's examples of civil disobedience (e.g., Shadrach, Meshach, and Abednego in Dan 3) and the insurrectionists' example of mob rule. Further, voter suppression laws—like those passed by Stop the Steal supporters in the Georgia and Texas legislatures in 2021 in response to unsupported allegations of fraud in the 2020 federal elections—are also calls for the prophet to preach. Such laws target wage-earning and minority voters, specifically seeking to disenfranchise them. The Voting Rights Act of 1965 did away with "poll taxes" that imposed financial burdens as a prerequisite to voting, mandating free and fair elections. Well, if polling places are disproportionately closed in wage-earning minority communities, necessitating that registrants take off from work and travel to other parts of town to vote, participating in the election is no longer free and is most certainly not fair. Those governmental actions necessitate prophetic responsiveness. Stated otherwise, the prophet must preach!

Well before the #MAGA political framework became popularized in the 2016 presidential election, the need for prophetic preaching was still apparent. In 2004, for example, there were human rights violations at the Abu Ghraib prison in Iraq, where foreign nationals were tortured by US soldiers. Those incidents necessitated a prophetic response. In 2002, there were also incidents of waterboarding prisoners at Guantanamo Bay, Cuba. Those incidents likewise necessitated a prophetic response. Indeed, just as incidents necessitating the church's prophetic response have occurred in the past, they will also most certainly occur in the future. It is therefore imperative that the church learns from its past in anticipation of its future. In following Jesus's example, the church is compelled to go further than piety. It must also address matters of politics!

At a time when the church had arguably done a Rip van Winkle and comfortably fallen asleep during the administration of Barack Obama, America's first Black president, Trump's abrasive political rhetoric and #MAGA politics and policies went to the heart of white nationalism by stoking racial tensions that returned America to a dark time—prior to the civil rights movement's hard-fought social advances—setting off an abrasive alarm that woke the church up!

As part of #MAGA's deliberate divisiveness during the 2016 election, Trump called Mexicans drug dealers, rapists, and murderers while simultaneously advocating for a ban on all Muslims entering the United States.[12] Consequently, well before the January 2017 presidential inauguration, the #MAGA cultural framework caused a reactionary political (and prophetic) fusion between progressive and feminist organizations along with progressive evangelical Christians wherein the church was determined to get political and have its say.

By the 2018 midterm elections, even left-leaning evangelical Christians had separated from the more traditional Religious Right in openly opposing the Christian nationalism that had become so widespread.[13] The church was again fully engaged in politics, as social circumstances necessitated that its prophetic leaders stand up. Stated otherwise, the church not only once again showed its concern with salvation in the kingdom to come but was again immersed in the struggle for social equity in the kingdom at hand.

Leading up to the 2020 presidential election, this trend continued with the aid of technology during the Covid-19 pandemic. Prophetic leaders like Reverends William J. Barber II and Liz Theoharis mobilized multitudes through the Poor People's Campaign: A National Call for Moral Revival, including multiple virtual and in-person events, while preparing caravans to protest at then senate majority leader Mitch McConnell's offices to oppose the confirmation of Trump's Supreme Court nominee Amy Coney Barrett.

Oppressive social circumstances necessitate prophetic action, usually beginning with prophetic preaching. In *Preaching as Resistance*, a prophetic work published in direct response to the Christian nationalism and rhetoric of racism so openly associated with the #MAGA political narrative, Phil Snider writes, "The most vital Christian preaching going on today quietly takes place week after week in local congregations, by everyday pastors committed to the hard work of justice and transformation in their particular contexts and communities."[14] Stated otherwise, the preachers who work to incorporate justice into their weekly sermons are pushing the powerful and prophetic narratives further. They lead their respective churches in getting political!

The Black Church Has Historically Responded to Social Injustice by Getting Political

In the image of Jesus, the Black church's history is replete with examples of political engagement by speaking truth to power as a voice for the socially marginalized. Since the African Methodist Episcopal Church's 1787 inception and its 1816 incorporation as an independent and autonomous ecclesial body, the Black church has been political by being at the forefront of social justice and resistance politics.[15] Richard Allen, the denomination's founder and first elected and consecrated bishop, led a Black exodus from Philadelphia's St. George's Methodist Episcopal Church (now St. George's United Methodist Church) in protest against discriminatory policies of racial segregation.[16] Denmark Vesey, a founder of the historic Emanuel AME Church in Charleston, South Carolina, led an 1812 slave rebellion.[17] Bishop Henry McNeal Turner, a liberationist clergyman and political organizer in Georgia, was appropriately described as "the most radical political voice in the nineteenth century."[18] It is therefore no surprise that the Black church would be at the forefront of the resistance politics that later launched the civil rights movement; the Black church was birthed in resistance politics.

Although there are different perspectives as to when the civil rights movement exactly began, it unquestionably started with the political resistance of the Black church. Some say the underlying case giving rise to the Supreme Court's famous decision in *Brown v. Board of Education* (1954) set things in place. Indeed, the underlying case began when Reverend Oliver Brown, a minister at St. Mark's AME Church in Topeka, Kansas, worked with the NAACP Legal Defense Fund to sue the board of education on behalf of his daughter Linda and all others similarly situated who were subjected to racial discrimination.[19] As a clergyperson in a liberationist faith tradition, Reverend Brown well understood that just as God does not discriminate between people based on race (Acts 10:34), humans should not discriminate against one another either.

Others argue the civil rights movement began with Rosa Parks's December 1, 1955, act of civil disobedience, refusing to give up her seat on a municipal bus and defying the segregation laws of the former capital of the Confederacy, as the Montgomery bus boycott began. Although Parks was not a member of the clergy, she was indeed a very active member of the AME Church and well trained in its resistance politics.[20] Regardless, however, of which event one considers to be the movement's genesis, the culmination of the two was the yearlong boycott that introduced the world to a young Reverend King.

Prophetic Preaching Led the Black Church into Politics!

Preaching influences congregations. In calling for a response to issues of social injustice, *prophetic* preaching invites congregations to become politically engaged with action, to address the issues articulated by preachers. As a young pastor who bloomed into a prophetic preacher, King influenced not only his individual congregation but also the church universal.

King arrived in Montgomery in 1954 and became Dexter Avenue's pastor. At the boycott's beginning, in December 1955, just over a year after his pastoral installation, King's powerful oration at Holt Street Baptist Church exemplified *prophetic preaching*. By using a synthesis of biblical and civil-religious rhetoric, his message of inclusion, rooted in Paul's New Testament theology of equality, likened African Americans' oppression in the South to the oppression suffered by the children of Israel throughout the Holy Bible.[21] Indeed, as the book of Exodus shows, as well as the gospel narratives describing the oppressive social conditions under which Jesus's ministry began, the children of Israel were consistently marginalized as a minority group. The same can be said of how Blacks have historically been marginalized in America. King's transformative speech at the onset of the yearlong boycott—an address filled with rhetorical tools developed in the Black church's preaching tradition—moved the Black church from pure piety into the protests of politics and created a pathway for the church universal to follow.

The Theology behind King's Prophetic Preaching

From the movement's early stages, in 1955 and 1956, through its successful passage of the Civil Rights Act of 1964 and the Voting Rights Act of 1965, King's prophetic preaching (and consequently the activism of the church) was undergirded by a suffering servant theology that focused on communal good instead of individualism. The theological underpinnings that supported this theology of sacrifice and suffering as part of the Black church's politicization were (1) evangelical liberalism, (2) the moral duty to disobey unjust laws, (3) love and equality, and (4) the suffering servant messianic theology. Each is addressed below.

Evangelical Liberalism

Evangelical liberalism is a philosophy that assumes Scripture requires the church's deference to the state and actively seeks social justice, especially in response to state-sponsored oppression. The philosophy is in direct contrast to the doctrine of evangelical conservatism that embraced a strict separation between the church and political issues.[22] For example, evangelical conservativism was used to support nineteenth-century slavery (Rom 13:1). King instead focused on human goodness and the church's necessary social role, which was foundational in the civil rights movement, as part of evangelical liberalism.

Indeed, several prophetic leaders in the Black church tradition helped shape American history, as thousands and thousands of African American churchgoers gained enough courage from their faith to defy unjust laws by participating in different types of protests while suffering beatings and even death in places like Selma and Montgomery, Alabama. The popular hymn "We Shall Overcome" became both a cry of defiance and a confession of faith. In underscoring how fundamental evangelical liberalism was to the Black church, Anthony E. Cook writes, "Given intrinsic human goodness, social institutions could and should be transformed to reflect more accurately the ideals of universal kinship and cooperation. An infallible scripture reflecting the static will of God could not justify social institutions like slavery and segregation."[23] King believed in intrinsic human goodness, and his embrace of evangelical liberalism led the church in fighting for good rather than standing idly by and allowing evil to have the day.

The Moral Duty to Disobey Unjust Laws

While incarcerated over Easter weekend in 1963, King wrote a treatise on civil disobedience in his famed "Letter from Birmingham City Jail." He responded to fellow clergy members' criticisms of his secular engagement and resistance to laws he deemed "unjust" by sharing,

> You express a great deal of anxiety over our willingness to break laws. This is certainly a legitimate concern. Since we so diligently urge people to obey the Supreme Court's decision of 1954 outlawing segregation in public schools, it is rather paradoxical to find us consciously breaking laws. One may well ask, "How can you advocate breaking some laws and obeying others?" The answer is found in the fact that there are two types of laws: there are just and there are unjust laws. I would agree with St. Augustine that "An unjust law is no law at all."[24]

Civil disobedience motivated faithful actors like the Freedom Riders in 1961 and the Bloody Sunday marchers in 1965. King also celebrated peaceful resistance to injustice in a November 1961 speech he gave at the annual meeting of the Fellowship for the Concerned. He shared that in responding to oppression, oppressed peoples can either acquiesce and simply accept injustice or respond with violence to combat the oppression. In rejecting those alternatives, he lauded the type of civil disobedience, or non-violent resistance, popularized in India by Mohandas Gandhi as a third option.[25]

King had a moral compulsion to disobey unjust laws because they could not be squared with what he considered to be God's law. He therefore advocated for reforms that were consistent with his view of the moral law based on the teachings of Jesus Christ. Indeed, the civil rights movement was designed to be an agent of change that would bring about moral reform.[26] King's prophetic leadership in civil disobedience was therefore motivated by his faith, just as were the dissident acts of Shadrach, Meshach, and Abednego (Dan 3).

Love and Equality

King's egalitarianism was based on the transformative love he showed his enemies. For example, when King's home was fire-bombed in January 1956, he addressed the crowd that gathered in front of his visibly damaged residence: "We must love our white brothers . . . no matter what they do to us. We must make them know that we love them. Jesus still cries out in words that echo across the centuries: 'Love your enemies. . . .' This is what we must live by. We must meet hate with love."[27] Love and equality were core philosophical components of King's leadership. He believed they were the most effective ways to fight injustice, because he knew the problem of racism would not be solved without lov-ing one's enemies. This love was an undergirding essence of his leadership during the civil rights movement because it went hand in hand with nonviolence.

Indeed, King's philosophical connection between love and nonviolence stands in direct contrast to the violence perpetrated by members of the church and their post–Civil War "religion of a Lost Cause" that justified violence against Blacks based on the Christian exceptionalism of white supremacy.[28]

The Redemptive Nature of Sacrificial Suffering

In directly building on his theology of love and equality, King also believed unmerited, sacrificial suffering was redemptive.

In an April 27, 1960, article for *Christian Century*, after being asked to share his views on suffering, King wrote, "My personal trials have also taught me the value of unmerited suffering. As my sufferings mounted, I soon realized that there were two ways that I could respond to my situation: either to react with bitterness or seek to transform the suffering into a creative force. I decided to follow the latter course. Recognizing the necessity of suffering I have to make of it a virtue. . . . I have lived these last few years with the conviction that unmerited suffering is redemptive."[29] This theology of redemptive suffering is arguably based on Isaiah's Fourth Servant Song (Isa 53:4–12). King's sentiment, one largely shared by dissident actors in the civil rights movement, was that Isaiah's prediction of a messiah who would redemptively suffer on behalf of others came to fruition in the unmerited suffering of Jesus the Christ. Since unmerited suffering is redemptive, King, therefore, viewed his trials and tribulations as being "Christlike."

For example, Bloody Sunday, March 7, 1965—when nonviolent marchers suffered significant attacks after crossing the Edmund Pettus Bridge, simply seeking the right to vote—illustrates redemptive suffering. On that infamous day, when Congressman John Lewis kneeled for prayer before being attacked by a combination of tear gas and an Alabama state trooper's multiple strikes to his skull, he had a sense of peace.[30] This peacefulness in the midst of protest illustrates that unmerited suffering is indeed redemptive when done for a cause greater than oneself. In the history of the church, there's no better example of this than the sacrifice Jesus made on Calvary.

These core fundamental tenants of evangelical liberalism, the moral duty to disobey unjust laws, love and equality, and sacrificial suffering as redemptive set a foundation for understanding the Black church's historic and prophetic entry into secular politics.

A More Contemporary Understanding of When the Church Gets Political

The Black church has a celebrated history of prophetic social action and political engagement. Eric L. McDaniel builds on that foundation and goes a step further in *Politics in the Pews* by establishing specific criteria to measure exactly *when* congregations "get political." Although McDaniel's research focuses on primarily Black churches, his logic is universally applicable.

In drawing from both qualitative and quantitative ethnographic research, through interviews with pastors and members of congregations in Detroit, Michigan, and Austin, Texas, McDaniel writes, "Specifically, a church becomes politically active when four conditions are met: the pastor is interested in involving his or her church in politics; the members are receptive to the idea of having a politically active church; the church itself is not restricted from having a presence in political matters; and the current political climate necessitates and allows political action."[31] In this section, I critique McDaniel's criteria by matching them against either historical or contemporary applications before offering a synthesizing conclusion to this chapter.

The Pastor Is Interested in Involving His or Her Church in Politics

A political church is a church holding political awareness and activity as salient pieces of its identity. By communicating a need for engagement in the community, beyond the four walls of the church edifice, a congregation forms a political identity. This happens when the pastor increases community awareness or encourages political (*not partisan*) involvement.[32]

Recent sociopolitical attempts to set back America's civil rights agenda have created an atmosphere where the requisite salience is as prevalent today as it was during the 1960s. In 2020, for example, after the horrific deaths of Ahmaud Arbery (killed while jogging in broad daylight by white neighborhood vigilantes, who literally hunted Arbery down and shot him) as well as Breonna Taylor and George Floyd (both killed by armed police officers amid a renewed #BlackLivesMatter movement that publicly spoke against the widespread killings of unarmed African Americans in a clear devaluation of Black life), Reverend Dr. Frederick D. Haynes, the senior pastor of Friendship-West Baptist Church in Dallas, Texas, displayed a huge "Black Lives Matter" sign on the front of his church edifice, drawing attention from the interstate, to deliberately influence public debate. Haynes, a minister with a celebrated history of prophetic preaching and political activism, was clear in showing that when social circumstances necessitate, the church should never shy away from politics.

Similarly, ministers serving congregations with prime geographic locations—including Reverend William H. Lamar, the senior pastor of Metropolitan AME Church in Washington, DC—also displayed "Black Lives Matter" signs, drawing the obvious ire of white supremacist actors who vandalized the sign after Trump's November 2020 defeat. Yours truly also continued sharing sermons on social justice and political participation through the lens of a prophetic preacher. As an example, on the Sunday that began early voting for the November 2020 elections in North Carolina, just before St. Joseph led a community-wide #SoulsToThePolls, a traditional rallying call in the Black church tradition where the politically minded pastor mobilizes faith communities to vote en masse, I compared America's broken state to Jerusalem during the Babylonian exile and suggested that voting was the only way to rebuild: "You see the trouble we're in, how Jerusalem [the United States] lies in ruins" (Neh 3:17).

These examples show that if pastors are interested in leading their congregations into political matters, there are more than ample opportunities to be engaged. Churches can be leaders in voter registration drives. Pastors and congregational leaders can provide public testimony on matters like redistricting if proposed maps do not seem fair or marginalize certain demographics. Congregations with sufficient resources can work with local governmental entities to address food insecurity by serving homeless populations and can also work with education officials to host both after-school tutorials and "Saturday schools" that offer both mentoring and support to supplement the academic curriculum, especially in areas like science, technology, engineering, and math (STEM).

Although I stayed clear of partisanship and did not publicly endorse any specific candidate during the November 2020 election cycle, I actively asked congregants to "get political" by voting. Members of the church cannot simply wait for salvation in the kingdom to come. Through the church, we must "save ourselves" from bad governance by voting and actively participating in political affairs in the kingdom at hand. Indeed, people should be informed on the relevant issues and vote in every election. As evidenced by the 2020 election returns, most Americans shared my position. More people voted in the November 2020 presidential election than at any other time in American history.

The Members Are Receptive to the Idea of Having a Politically Active Church

Although a pastor's willingness to operate in the political realm is one thing, that ability will be significantly limited without the church membership being receptive to political activity. Stated otherwise, congregational receptivity resembles congregational support. In expounding on this, McDaniel argues that the church's sociopolitical environment will influence members' attitudes and actions.[33]

I am blessed to serve a congregation that delights in a well-deserved reputation of being publicly engaged in political leadership in North Carolina's fight for human equality for more than 150 years. St. Joseph's members and pastors have served and continue serving in both publicly elected and appointed offices. In fact, many of the congregation's current members remain politically engaged, especially in the #MAGA climate, where this fight has again become so fundamental. Moreover, in using their resources wisely and considering the ill effects of gentrification, St. Joseph's members have gotten political by working with nonprofits to ensure the community has affordable housing. The members are political; they lead civic organizations, represent the congregation in voter registration drives, and serve as poll workers to ensure there are no undue challenges to registrants who attempt to cast ballots.

The environment's influence on a congregation is the most important determinant of whether it will be receptive to a pastor's political participation.[34] For example, during the Trump administration, one could hardly watch the news or read periodicals without noting active faith-based, protest resistance in responding to environmental conditions. In addition to the 2020 killings of Breonna Taylor and George Floyd—both at the hands of law enforcement officers—congregations had to wrestle with the political question of whether America had a culture of systemic racism or simply a few individual racists.

The year before, in August 2019, congregations had to respond to the racially motivated shootings of Mexicans and Mexican Americans outside a Walmart in El Paso, Texas, while still dealing with the national aftermath of xenophobic hatred following the Confederate monument removals that fueled the infamous August 2017 white supremacist Unite the Right rally in Charlottesville, Virginia. If nothing else, the #MAGA narrative proved that environmental conditions can very much necessitate the church's prophetic response and consequential political involvement if members are receptive to political engagement.

As final edits were being completed for this book, and as the 2022 midterm elections were in full swing, St. Joseph's members showed a sincere receptiveness to having a politically active church by organizing another #SoulsToThePolls, a faith-based event in association with Sunday morning worship wherein the congregation addresses the social justice issues of the day and sojourns to a designated early voting precinct to vote in bulk with other members of the community. On Sunday, October 23, 2022, St. Joseph welcomed keynote speaker Marc H. Morial, the president and CEO of the National Urban League, in an interfaith collaborative with Rabbi Matthew Soffer and the Judea Reform Synagogue, along with many elected officials and candidates for public office, as both congregations showed political activeness.

The Church Itself Is Not (Socially) Restricted from Having a Presence in Political Matters

In addition to its ability to unite people and defend their rights, the church has also received criticism for its lack of action. Over the last several decades, for example, the Religious Right has narrowly defined a "justice agenda" by primarily framing two issues for debate: abortion and gay marriage. The Black church has not been immune from this deliberately narrow social framing either.

Inasmuch as church politicization originates as a part of self-identity, where the pastor and then the members decide to become politically engaged, the argument can be made that the internal dynamics of megachurches often prevent political activity, even in a political environment. Because megachurches cast a wide net in recruiting members and often embrace prosperity theology—focusing on the accumulation of material items instead of the practice of prophetic resistance—their attempt at universal popularity will inevitably water down any political message. Except for the few megachurches that embraced the Christian nationalism of the #MAGA narrative, prosperity preachers almost never engage in politics.[35]

The Current Political Climate Both Necessitates and Allows Political Action

Prior to the Montgomery bus boycott, King was enjoying parish ministry and *did not* attempt to make any waves. During the summer and fall of 1955, he was engaged in a more philosophical style of preaching, rarely attacking the problem of racism in Montgomery.[36] *After* the boycott began, however, he led his individual, primarily Black congregation—and ultimately the church universal—into political activism. Just as social conditions in King's Montgomery and the American South necessitated the church's prophetic response back then, the same must be said of the church in recent years.

In chronicling the organized formation of a Religious Left and describing the political ascent of prophetic leaders like Barber and Reverend Traci Blackmon, in *American Prophets: The Religious Roots of Progressive Politics and the Ongoing Fight for the Soul of the Country*, Jack Jenkins describes Blackmon as stepping behind a pulpit in Charlottesville on August 11, 2017, to speak at a counterdemonstration to the Unite the Right rally by arguing for the church to exercise prophetic leadership. She shared, "When violence and hatred are flourishing, it is necessary that love show up. . . . When hatred is all around, when violence is the language of the day, when laws lack compassion and churches lose their way, then we who believe in freedom, we who believe in God . . . we must question: *Where have all the prophets gone?*"[37] With a theological core reminiscent of King's leadership more than a half century before, Blackmon's response again showed that the church gets political when circumstances necessitate action.

Conclusion

This chapter raised the foundational question, "When does the church get political?" In answering, there are parallels between the oppressive conditions that necessitated clergy leadership in the twentieth-century civil rights movement and the oppressive conditions that birthed an ecclesial and interfaith response to the more recent #MAGA political narrative. Jesus's ministry and the Black church were both birthed to address salvation *and* social justice. Stated otherwise, the church was born in politics. To place this reality in ecclesial leadership terms, the church's priestly work is not in competition with its prophetic responsibility. Instead, those two leadership domains should complement each other if the church is to live out its calling. To again paraphrase King, anything else makes for a dryasdust religion.

Most progressive Christian political organizing movements have been *reactive* as opposed to *proactive*. Inasmuch as conservative evangelical Christians have had a more sustained relationship with Republicans, dating back to Ronald Reagan's 1980 political alliance with the Religious Right, on the more progressive side, faith leaders' alliance with Joe Biden in 2020 was much more so a reaction to Donald Trump. In moving forward, therefore, insofar as progressive coalitions organizing around faith and faith-based issues is still in the early stages, the church should not just *get* political but *stay* political by remaining engaged with affairs of the state.

Rather than doing another Rip van Winkle and becoming complacent amid cooperation, more denominations should follow the examples of those who have staffed positions for clergy and laity to serve in *political*, but *not partisan*, capacities. For example, before becoming the inaugural executive director of Faith in Public Life and serving as chair of the White House Council on Faith and Neighborhood Partnerships, Reverend Jennifer Butler represented the Presbyterian Church (USA) in the field of international human rights at the United Nations. Similarly, in addition to her pastoral service in Missouri, Reverend Blackmon serves as the executive minister of Justice and Witness Ministries for the United Church of Christ. Further, as more of an ecumenical social justice think tank, Reverend Dr. Katharine Rhodes Henderson, a Presbyterian minister, previously led the progressive Auburn Seminary, an institution that is currently being led by Reverend Dr. Emma Jordan-Simpson, a Baptist minister. As I think about the future of faith-based political organizing, in again raising the question of if the church gets political, it always has been and must always be so!

With all the realities of politics, America has fallen into a state of dramatic polarization. This brings up the question of the role of reconciliation. It's a theological term that is inherently political. Inasmuch as Jesus was political, Jesus also left the ministry of reconciliation to the church. Now, to the work of reconciliation in America.

2

RECKONING, RECONCILIATION, AND REPAIR

So if anyone is in Christ, there is a new creation; everything old has passed away; see, everything has become new! All this from God, who reconciled us to himself through Christ, and has given us the ministry of reconciliation; that is, in Christ God was reconciling the world to himself, not counting their trespasses against them, and entrusting the message of reconciliation to us.

—2 Corinthians 5:17–19

Zacchaeus stood there and said to the Lord, ". . . if I have defrauded anyone of anything, I will pay back four times as much."

—Luke 19:8

April 20, 2021, was a day of reckoning in the United States, and it had everything to do with race.

In the truest sense of the word, *reckoning* has to do with accountability, like the settling of accounts. On this strange day, in many regards, the American criminal justice system began to settle its account with Black America after it failed to provide justice in so many previous cases. Amid a rebirthed #BlackLivesMatter (BLM) movement in 2020, the system had failed to provide justice after the brutal killings of Breonna Taylor in Louisville, Kentucky, and Ahmaud Arbery in New Brunswick, Georgia. This is the same system that failed to provide justice several years earlier, when the original BLM movement began, after police officers brutally killed Eric Garner in Staten Island, New York, and Philando Castile in Falcon Heights, Minnesota.

The fact that the criminal justice system had failed to provide *any justice* in those cases—as well as many others—was the reason so many had pause on April 20, 2021. All of America was waiting for a Minneapolis, Minnesota, jury's verdict for the murder trial of Derek Chauvin, a disgraced white police officer who mercilessly killed George Floyd, an unarmed Black man, by keeping his knee on Floyd's neck for more than nine minutes. Although the entire world had seen a televised trial presenting crystal clear evidence that Chauvin used excessive force and unnecessarily killed Floyd on May 25, 2020, almost a year later, so many people *still* had pause because of a concern that there would not be justice.

I had pause based on my personal experiences; I have had these feelings several times in my personal life. I still remember the feeling I had in college when I learned that the officers who had brutally beaten Rodney King in Los Angeles—notwithstanding videotaped evidence—were found "not guilty." I also had pause because I had felt the same feeling several years later when I learned the grand jury decided not to indict the rogue white police officer who shot down and killed Michael Brown, an unarmed Black teenager, in Ferguson, Missouri. To therefore avoid yet another feeling of disappointment and further disillusionment with the concept of justice in America, I can safely say that I, along with many others, simply had pause.

April 20, 2021, however, was different. As a day of *reckoning*— in the truest sense of the word—the jury found Chauvin guilty of killing Floyd. While some quickly proclaimed the verdict was justice, political commentator Bakari Sellers was correct when he described it *not as justice* but as a move toward accountability.[1] Sellers's comments were providential because they emphasized the verdict did not solve the problem of systemic racism in America. His words were proven true when the very next day, on April 21, 2021, a group of white police officers shot down and killed still *another* unarmed Black man, Andrew Brown Jr., in Elizabeth City, North Carolina.

Inasmuch as America has a well-documented history with the issue of racism and insofar as the Chauvin verdict was a day of reckoning and a step toward accountability, the question must be raised as to whether America is prepared to move toward reconciliation. Assuming so, the corollary question must be to what extent it is willing to go to repair the damage racism has done, recognizing that the hard work of reconciliation is a ministry Jesus left to the church (2 Cor 5:17–19) and that the church's work should be an exemplar to society at large.

The Christian Duty to Repair

The word *reconciliation*—the idea that requires forgiveness by the oppressed and a reciprocal repentance by the oppressors (2 Cor 5:18–19)—came into the American lexicon from Scripture, primarily from its varied uses in Paul's letters, and was popularized in the secular context by the 1980s South African Truth and Reconciliation Commission. In *Called to Reconciliation: How the Church Can Model Justice, Diversity, and Inclusion*, I define it as "an ongoing spiritual process involving forgiveness, repentance, and justice that restores broken relationships and systems to reflect God's original intention for all creation to flourish."[2] Since it deals with repairing broken relationships, the concept of *reparations*—a form of reparative justice that has to do with systemic repair for wrongs perpetrated against victims—must also be a part of the conversation. Indeed, the idea of reparations has biblical origins too.

As God was preparing to emancipate the Israelites from slavery in Egypt, Pharaoh became penitent for his actions (Exod 10:16–17). Before the Israelites left captivity, God had Moses instruct them to ask for gold and silver *before* the exodus so they would not leave empty-handed (see, e.g., Exod 3:22; 11:2; 12:35–36). Scripture thus supports the idea that repentance should also include repair (Luke 19:8). For example, after George Floyd's May 25, 2020, murder, several municipalities began serious conversations about reparations as a form of reparative justice for Black Americans. In fact, in my now hometown, Durham, North Carolina, the city announced concrete goals toward reparations, as offered by its racial equity task force.[3] These are obvious attempts to repair the damage done by the ongoing effects of racism and race-based governmental policies.

The concept of *reparative* justice requires the church to address the issue of white supremacy and its ongoing effects as part of the reconciliation paradigm. There is a proprietary nature to the term *reparations*. Consequently, *notwithstanding the Christian duty to repair*, the payment of *reparations* to African Americans is really within the province of the federal government, the entity that is both culpable for the injuries African Americans have sustained and capable of paying reparations to repair them.[4] Indeed, the payment of reparations by the federal government is not a novel concept. In previous instances, after injurious acts of oppression, the federal government paid reparations to Japanese Americans for forced internment during World War II, to victims of the Nazi Holocaust, and to Native Peoples who were forcibly removed from their land, with families.[5] In the case of African Americans, however, reparations have never been paid for the generational injuries caused to the families of those who were previously enslaved.

Although President Abraham Lincoln approved of reparations in concept, after his assassination, President Andrew Johnson, a southerner from Tennessee, pulled the economic rug from beneath the feet of the formerly enslaved during the early part of Reconstruction. Reverend Dr. Martin Luther King Jr. referred to the American government's failure to give reparations when he talked about "the check" that was returned for insufficient funds during his famous August 28, 1963, "I Have a Dream" speech.[6] Using the image of the Bible's Exodus narrative, Blacks have repeatedly asked for gold and silver. Unlike the Israelite emancipation with Moses, however, reparations for African Americans have never been paid. While reparative justice was appropriate with respect to other subjugated ethnicities, *now*, more than 250 years later, "the check" is still being returned for insufficient funds.[7]

The Secular Lens of Reparative Justice: What Happened to the Promise of Forty Acres and a Mule?

If the church is to provide prophetic leadership in the ministry of reconciliation that Jesus left to it (2 Cor 5:17–19), it cannot be afraid of discussing reparations. Although the payment of reparations is squarely within the province of the federal government, as the entity both *capable* of making payments and *culpable* for the systemic harms suffered by African Americans, church-based ministries are correct in advocating for reparations and doing their part to support them.

Georgetown University, a ministry of the Catholic Church, and Virginia Theological Seminary, a ministry of the Episcopal Church, have already led the way through their efforts in repairing both broken systems and broken relationships by publicly showing their support for reparations and illustrating the Christian duty to repair.[8] To better understand that duty, especially as it relates to the Black and white racial reconciliation paradigm in America, prophetic leaders should learn about the federal government's broken promise to repair the damage done by the institution of slavery in the United States.

In the wake of the Civil War and after President Lincoln's Emancipation Proclamation, officials from the federal government consulted with a group of African American ministers, including Reverend Garrison Frazier, to fashion a remedy to help create economic stability in Black communities. The ministers recommended and the federal government approved land allocations for the former slaves so their families could grow their own food, manage their own property, and have economic independence.[9] This widely popularized governmental promise was known as "forty acres and a mule."

In July 1865, while serving as the head of the Freedmen's Bureau, former Union general Oliver Otis Howard, who would later be the namesake of Howard University, issued Circular 13 to fully authorize the lease of forty-acre plots from abandoned plantations to the newly freed families. After Lincoln's assassination, however, in a twist of fate, the new president, Johnson, rescinded Howard's order and commanded the army to throw tens of thousands of freed people off the land and return it to plantation owners.[10] Blacks received nothing.

Exodus begins by indicating that a *new* pharaoh, who did not know Joseph, came to power and reigned over Egypt. He despised the Israelites and assigned taskmasters to lord over them and make their lives miserable (Exod 1:11, 13–14). In 1865, after the *new* president came to power, he knew nothing of America's promise of forty acres and a mule and had no concept of reparative justice. Johnson seemed to despise Black Americans, just as the new pharaoh despised the Israelites.

In 1876, at the end of Reconstruction, after President Ulysses S. Grant declined to seek reelection, America endured the contentious election between Rutherford Hayes and Samuel Tilden. As neither candidate had a clear majority in the Electoral College, Republican and Democratic congressional leaders engineered a deal that became known as the Compromise of 1877. Democrats conceded to Hayes's election among contested Southern states in the Electoral College, and Republicans agreed to withdraw federal troops from the South. This compromise ended Reconstruction and ushered in the period of redemption, a time leading to Jim Crow segregation, when white vigilante lynch mobs resorted to violence because they wanted *their country* back. This dynamic in American history is no different from the Exodus narrative, after the Israelites were emancipated and Pharaoh had a case of buyer's remorse.

The writer of Exodus records, "When the king of Egypt was told that the people had fled, the minds of Pharaoh and his officials were changed toward the people and they said, 'What have we done, letting Israel leave our service?'" (Exod 14:5). The writer goes on to share, "So he had his chariot made ready, and took his army with him. . . . The Lord hardened the heart of Pharaoh king of Egypt and he pursued the Israelites, who were going out boldly" (Exod 14:6–8). In other words, Pharaoh essentially said, "We want our country back," just as white vigilante groups like the Ku Klux Klan did in 1877, when the Reconstruction era abruptly came to an end.

America's promises of reparative justice for African Americans never came to fruition. As a great irony, however, with a nod toward repair, rather than following through and compensating the former slaves for the uncompensated labor they furnished prior to emancipation, the federal government instead compensated certain *slave owners*, up to $300, for each of their freed slaves.[11]

The Sacred Lens of Reparative Justice

In Luke's story of Zacchaeus, we see an evolution where Jericho's chief tax collector—one who Luke describes as rich—repents from his wrongdoings and promises to repair the damage he's done.

The tax collection system in the Roman province of Judea was fraught with opportunities for corruption. Tax collectors typically prepaid the Roman government for taxes and tolls to be collected, allowing them to add surcharges and tax their territories as they deemed appropriate, often leading to excessive financial profits from gaming the system. In well-populated and well-traveled areas, like Jericho, tax collectors would overcharge passersby and confiscate their goods, with the Roman government often turning a blind eye to the inherent corruption. Zacchaeus had mastered this system and risen through its ranks, advancing to the status of a *chief* tax collector. In other words, he had done a whole lot of wrong to a whole lot of people and profited immensely because of his corruption.

Like slaveholders who profited from the institution of slavery, Jim Crow election officials who charged poll taxes that were excessive and often cost prohibitive, and property accessors who participated in restrictive covenants that discriminated against minorities, Zacchaeus's actions as a governmental official caused immeasurable harm to a host of unnamed people. He had a day of moral reckoning when Jesus passed through Jericho and helped Zacchaeus see his wrong. He then committed to making restitution (or repair) for his wrongdoings by paying *four times* as much as he had taken (19:8).

Zacchaeus's promise was indeed an act of contrition toward reparative justice, but it was also grounded in Jewish law. Indeed, he had double shame not only for profiting from such a corrupt system but for also causing harm to his fellow Jews. His move toward restorative justice was, therefore, not so much an act of magnanimity but instead rooted in his understanding of Hebrew Scriptures (see, e.g., Lev 6:1–7; Num 5:5–7). Inasmuch as Hebrew Scriptures undergird Christian practices and clearly influence the New Testament story of Zacchaeus, they also show that the Bible supports restorative justice and, in the case of the government causing harm to others, the payment of reparations for the harm caused.

In Luke's parable of the Good Samaritan, there is no governmental actor and no payment of reparations. There still is, however, the practice of reparative justice, as a Samaritan empathically sees the harm done to the proverbial "Other" and seeks to repair it. Much like the white descendants of those who oppressed and marginalized Blacks and other minorities or financially benefited from oppressive institutions and institutional practices that were governmentally sanctioned, the Samaritan in Luke's parable isn't *personally* responsible for the victim's injury. In the spirit of the recognized duty to repair, however, the Samaritan looks past racial and ethnic differences and engages in a ministry of repair. Moreover, as Jesus invokes the Old Testament command to love your neighbor as yourself (Luke 10:27; Lev 19:18), he also teaches a lesson on race relations that would benefit us all in the United States, as biblical readers focus on the parable's central question, "*Who* is my neighbor?" (Luke 10:29; emphasis added).

Although this parable is popularly referred to as that of the *Good* Samaritan, the writer of Luke never actually uses that descriptive term. Readers have deemed the Samaritan as "good" because of his actions. In sharing this celebrated parable about an unidentified man going down the road from Jerusalem to Jericho, Jesus tells of him falling victim to robbers and being left half dead (10:30). It's then that Jesus tells of three passersby, and it is the most unlikely of them, the Samaritan, who stops and engages in repair.

The first passerby, described as a priest, sees the unidentified man and goes to the other side of the road (10:31). Jesus's implication, in talking to fellow Jews about an unnamed traveler in the Judean province, is that both the victim *and* the priest are Jewish. Moreover, in describing the second passerby as a Levite, the reader is made to expressly understand that he is a Jewish descendant of the tribe of Levi. The Levite goes to the other side of the road, just as did the priest (10:32). It therefore appears that in initially answering the question, "Who is my neighbor?" Jesus makes the point that neither geography nor ethnicity should define our conceptualization of what it means to be a "neighbor."

The third passerby, *the Samaritan*—someone of a mixed ethnic ancestry who belongs to a racial group where enmity is typical between them and Jews—is the one who is emphatically moved with pity and engages in the ministry of reconciliation and the practice of repair (10:34–36). Placed in the contemporary context, Jesus shows us that although there has never been a sustained conciliatory relationship between Blacks and whites in America, we can indeed be "neighbors" if we're willing to move past stereotypes and divisions and be empathically connected with the Other. This Samaritan is regarded as *good* because he engages in racial reconciliation while providing an example of reparative justice. Indeed, given the evolving nature of the reconciliation conversation in America and the continual evidence of how white supremacy has and continues to adversely impact people of African descent, the practice of reparative justice must be a part of any serious dialogue on reconciliation.

Race and Reconciliation in America

The dialogue on racial reconciliation in America really began in the social unrest after King's April 4, 1968, assassination and has continued to evolve. As work toward reconciliation became more popular, there was a great paradox in the church because those who most adamantly opposed post–civil rights movement efforts to create diverse communities were also members of the church. Opposing freedom while being a Christian is possible because there is a difference between *integration* and *reconciliation*. While the former has to do with racial minorities being legally accepted into America's mainstream, the latter is really a fundamentally Christian practice.[12] Moreover, insofar as reconciliation is distinctively Christian, in the context of America's remedial efforts at dismantling racism, there is a fundamental difference between reconciliation and equity. Whereas reconciliation seeks to repair broken relationships while simultaneously finding commonality among human beings who were created in the image of God, equity is secular. America's efforts at racial equity seek to remedy the structural racism deeply embedded in America's culture and institutions.

In contemporary ministries, reconciliation is the expressly stated work of mainline communions like the Evangelical Lutheran Church and United Methodist Church. With a nod toward corporate America's post–George Floyd embrace of diversity, under the leadership of Presiding Bishop Michael B. Curry (the Episcopal Church's first African American to serve in said capacity), the denomination's website expressly states, "As the Episcopal Branch of the Jesus Movement, we dream and work to foster Beloved Communities where all people may experience dignity and abundant life and see themselves and others as beloved children of God."[13] Stated otherwise, the ministry of reconciliation seeks to establish siblings in Christ, as opposed to racialized enemies. This is the work of Jesus's church.

In W. E. B. Du Bois's classic *The Souls of Black Folk*, he famously argues that the problem of twentieth-century America was the color line, or divisions based on race.[14] Indeed, "in the American caste system, the signal of rank is what we call race, the division of humans on the basis of their appearance."[15] This statement remains true, as evidenced by the ongoing existence of white supremacy manifesting through things like police brutality and voter suppression legislation in states like Georgia and Texas as well as North Carolina, where the US Fourth Circuit Court of Appeals infamously ruled an omnibus law was unconstitutional because it targeted African American voters "with almost surgical precision."[16] Because America's problem with race has been ubiquitous, race *and racism* have been foundational parts of America since its founding.

The Concept of Race

Race in the United States is nothing more than a social construct.[17] Moreover, race and racial identities are nothing more than embodiments of the political, social, and moral choices people have lived through in maintaining structural relationships.[18] The conceptualization of race is, therefore, "an evolving social idea that was created to legitimize racial inequality and protect white advantage."[19] This is the core of *white supremacy*, a way of organizing based on race where society determines who and who not to value.[20] Indeed, America's race-based classifications have been used to justify *racism*, the systemic practices and beliefs adopted by whites, and used against people of color, to marginalize and minimalize while engaging in discrimination.

America's history of categorizing people in racialized terms began with the economic benefits of slavery. Distinctions among the various African peoples trapped in the transatlantic slave trade were inconsequential to their enslavers. The enslaved Africans were regarded as inferior and simply called "Black," a name based solely on skin color. The opposite of "Black," in terms of class, economic stability, and access to resources, of course, became "white." Consequently, as Eddie S. Glaude Jr. writes in *Democracy in Black: How Race Still Enslaves the American Soul*, "The social function of Whiteness was, in a word, supremacy."[21] Racial identities in America have always been associated with the socially manufactured benefits that accompany them. Racial classifications are, therefore, only social constructs that seek to empower certain classes of people and marginalize others while serving as the antithesis of reconciliation.

Contextualizing Reconciliation in America

A legitimate question can be raised as to whether *racial reconciliation* is an oxymoron, given the fact that America has never enjoyed a time where racial harmony existed, such to reconcile groups who have never enjoyed a conciliatory relationship.[22] Given America's history of social dichotomy, especially in the context of race, and since reconciliation is a Christian practice, reconciliation must be more about taking the journey than reaching a particular destination. It is God's invitation to participate in a developing relationship, like the process of an ongoing search.[23]

Americans on the journey have made both forward and backward steps. Most importantly, however, the journey is ongoing, as part of a ministry Jesus left to the church (2 Cor 5:19). The American reconciliation journey invites us to reject xenophobia and embrace the proverbial "Other" as a sibling in Christ. Reconciliation is also an opportunity to reject unconscious bias, a phenomenon that plagues so much of society. The real meaning of reconciliation, as emanating from Scripture, goes well beyond the limitations of race in that it is extremely broad and multifaceted. In moving from its very theological to its very practical applications, the contextualization of reconciliation moves full circle to *include race*, and in the framework of America, reconciliation must also include repair.

The conceptualization of what is "to be reconciled is salvific, social, and civil."[24] Although the threefold classifications are theological, they are also very much political in that they relate to social structures and affairs of the state. Consequently, in considering America's historic intermingling of race and partisan politics, reconciliation is again a part of the American narrative of race.

Salvific Reconciliation

Salvific reconciliation specifically deals with humanity being reconciled in its relationship with God *through* Jesus. Consider the following scripture from Paul: "For if while we were enemies, we were reconciled to God, through the death of his Son, much more surely, having been reconciled, will we be saved by his life. But more than that, we even boast in God through our Lord Jesus Christ, through whom we have now received reconciliation" (Rom 5:10–11).

Salvific reconciliation is similar in some regards to a penal substitution theory, whereby Christ literally pays the price for human sin. Stated otherwise, as I sometimes like to share as an acronym when preaching, Christians are saved by GRACE: God's riches at Christ's expense. This is the essence of salvific reconciliation; the individual is restored (reconciled) in relationship to God through the sacrificial suffering of Jesus.

Salvific reconciliation says that Jesus paid the price for us all. When preaching about my theology of unmerited grace, I often refer to salvific reconciliation by saying, "We can't pay for it, because we can't afford it. We can't earn it, because we'll mess things up almost every time. All we have to do is accept it as the free and unmerited gift we receive from God because of Jesus's suffering." Indeed, salvific reconciliation is at the heart of atonement theology. Individual humans are reconciled in their relationship with God *through* Jesus.

Social Reconciliation

As a direct derivative of or outgrowth from salvific reconciliation's focus on the individual's relationship with God, *social reconciliation* deals with group dynamics in how classes of people interplay with one another. Black brothers and sisters are equal to white brothers and sisters, just as straight brothers and sisters are equal to gay brothers and sisters. Men are equal to women, just as the wealthy are equal to the poor. Accordingly, in close connection with salvific reconciliation, a belief that humans are saved *through* Jesus, *social* reconciliation says all human beings are equal to one another *because of* Jesus. God does not recognize humanity's social divisions (Acts 10:34). Simply put, humans are both reconciled to God through Jesus and reconciled to one another because of Jesus.

The communal focus of social reconciliation stems directly from the individual focus of salvific reconciliation in moving toward a more equal treatment of others.[25] Social reconciliation leads one to rhetorically ask, "Now that I am saved, so what? How am I supposed to treat others?" In other words, after one is saved, they should become an ambassador of Christ (2 Cor 5:18–20). This means showing others Christ's liberating love and acceptance.

Inasmuch as salvific reconciliation focuses on the individual, because social reconciliation is communal, it requires several things of members within respective communities, as humans seek to live out the ministry of reconciliation Jesus left to the church (2 Cor 5:18). At a minimum, social reconciliation requires (1) the equal treatment of others, (2) forgiveness for previous acts, and (3) repentance from the one who is forgiven. As further explained in the succeeding paragraphs, in the American context, the reconciliation paradigm presupposes certain power dynamics, including a dominant class that has historically engaged in subjugating and a marginalized class that has been subjugated.

While the first element, the equal treatment of others, places all social and ethnic groups on the same playing field, the second and third elements, forgiveness and repentance, denote a history of dominant and marginalized classes, as exemplified by the narrative of white supremacy in America.

1. Social Reconciliation Requires the Equal Treatment of Others

As a scriptural basis for *social reconciliation*, a perspective that envisions diverse peoples living as equals, consider Paul's letter to the church at Galatia and the egalitarian nature of the following scripture: "As many of you as were baptized into Christ have clothed yourselves with Christ. There is no longer Jew or Greek, there is no longer slave or free, there is no longer male or female; for all of you are one in Christ Jesus" (Gal 3:27–28).

This liberating verse speaks to an interpersonal ethic of equality in relationships because of Jesus, promoting racial (Jews and gentiles), societal (free and slave), and sexual (female and male) oneness in Christ. It also speaks to a narrative of atonement and reconciliation that begins with the crucified Christ, moving to unite both Jews and gentiles. Accordingly, Galatians 3 provides an express scriptural basis to show that because there is equality within the body of Christ, acts of racism, classism, and sexism cannot comport with Scripture. The egalitarian-like theology of equality that is at the heart of social reconciliation requires that all peoples be treated equally.

In further contextualizing Paul's theology of equality in social reconciliation, in addition to Galatians 3, also consider Paul's rejection of social hierarchy in addressing abuses of the Lord's Supper (1 Cor 11:17–22). As an initial matter, the practice of observing the Lord's Supper back then was not like the liturgical and sacramental practice we observe today. Instead, the observation of the Lord's Supper was more like a common meal that was shared in someone's private home. The meal was intended to be a true communal place of social equality.

With a contextual appreciation of the practice of the Lord's Supper, we can also see that Paul wrote the Corinthian correspondence because of social divisions (1 Cor 1:11). He expressly addresses how the Corinthians didn't recognize their shared commonality as baptized members of the church (3:3–23). This was problematic for Paul because hierarchical social practices were the very antithesis of the equality he believed Christians shared after baptism.

In following a caste system, more privileged members of the Corinthian church would eat first, receiving more and better food than those who were less privileged.[26] In expressing his disdain for this practice, Paul advocates for equality: "For when the time comes to eat, each of you goes ahead with your own supper, and one goes hungry and another becomes drunk. What! Do you not have homes to eat and drink in? Or do you show contempt for the church of God and humiliate those who have nothing? What should I say to you? Should I commend you? In this matter I do not commend you!" (11:21–22). Paul's lack of commendation shows obvious displeasure with social practices that do not promote equality within the church.

2. Social Reconciliation Requires Forgiveness

In thinking about what reconciliation really is, as part of a journey all Christians are invited to take, it is "an ongoing spiritual process involving forgiveness, repentance, and justice that restores broken relationships and systems to reflect God's original intention for all creation to flourish."[27] This definition acknowledges some of the horrific roles the church has played in promoting racial *injustice* and the necessity of forgiveness in moving past racism.

After the fall of apartheid in South Africa, Bishop Desmond Tutu was appointed to chair the South African Truth and Reconciliation Commission. In his book *No Future without Forgiveness*, Tutu chronicles his experiences and describes how important forgiveness is for true reconciliation to occur. He notes that on April 27, 1994, the day Nelson Mandela was inaugurated as the president of South Africa, Mandela was an agent of reconciliation. For him, this included inviting his former white jailer to his inauguration as an honored guest.[28] Mandela's magnanimity shows how crucial forgiveness is on the journey to reconciliation.

As a member of a socially subjugated class who very well understands the hard work forgiveness requires, I acknowledge that forgiveness means wiping the slate clean and forgiving others for their transgressions, just as God forgives us for ours. Another Black man and minister who recognizes and accepts this same challenge as part of the Christian's duty of forgiveness is Anthony Thompson, the surviving spouse of one of the brutally slain Emanuel Nine, those faithful Bible study attendees who were killed by a racist white assassin on June 17, 2015, at Mother Emanuel AME Church in Charleston, South Carolina.

In *Called to Forgive,* Thompson details his pain and emotional disgust after his wife's murder while also describing his rejection of *partial forgiveness.* Instead, he encourages Christians to engage in *biblical forgiveness* by noting, "It doesn't come in baby steps, or stages. It must be all-encompassing, all-forgiving, completely erasing the terrible debt owed to us by a vicious other, no matter how horrible the crime."[29] The type of biblical forgiveness Thompson advocates is crucial: not only does it require Christians to be Christlike (Luke 23:34), but it also empowers the forgiver because the offender no longer has emotional power due to the offense.

Similarly, in the wake of the May 14, 2022, targeted race massacre at a grocery store in a primarily African America area of Buffalo, New York—after the assassin proudly revealed that he planned his attack based on the high concentration of African Americans living in the store's zip code—a local minister was interviewed and spoke about the importance of forgiveness and prayer for such a sick demonic person. The work of and requisites for reconciliation are obviously not easy. Indeed, they *are not* for the faint of heart. In the true spirit of Christianity, however, if followers of Jesus are to be "Christlike," we should all remember Jesus's words of forgiveness as he was being crucified: "Father forgive them, for they do not know what they are doing" (Luke 23:34). With Christ as an exemplar, the hard work of forgiveness is an essential part of the reconciliation paradigm.

3. Social Reconciliation Requires Repentance and Repair

Although repentance is a part of social reconciliation, its focus is not immediately communal. In America's social context, repentance must begin with members of the dominant power group introspectively acknowledging the omnipotent nature of white supremacy while also demonstrating a willingness to outwardly change the enduring consequences of a class structure that has benefited "whiteness" since 1619, when the institution of chattel slavery began in America. Further, in addition to repentance from members of the dominant class, reconciliation also requires deliberate work to repair broken relationships, as seen in Luke's story of Zacchaeus (Luke 19:1–10).

Social factions can be marked by racism or innate prejudices. In many instances, however, social factions can result from unconscious bias, a phenomenon where our preconceived ideas and prejudices about "Others" manifest through our thoughts and actions. Consider Peter. In Acts 10, he demonstrates a rejection of this type of bias only *after* he begins the work of taking the journey toward racial reconciliation. Although a devout Jew, Peter embraces Cornelius, a gentile, and realizes by divine revelation that prejudice toward gentiles is inconsistent with God's intention of bringing racially and ethnically diverse people together. After accepting God's invitation to take a reconciliation journey, Peter speaks to them: "I truly understand that God shows to partiality, but in every nation anyone who fears him and does what is right is acceptable to him" (Acts 10:34–35). Given the well-documented enmity between Jews and gentiles, Acts 10 provides a model for Blacks and whites proving there *can* be reconciliation today, even without a conciliatory history.

Civil Reconciliation

In connecting the ethic of social reconciliation with a manifestation of prophetic leadership, the result is *civil reconciliation*. When prophetic leaders seek to institutionalize the concept of social reconciliation (equality *because of* Jesus) within secular systems of justice by demanding civil change, we see civil reconciliation. When King and his clergy-led resistance movement demanded the Civil Rights Act of 1964 and the Voting Rights Act of 1965, they were exemplars of civil reconciliation.

Just as the public protest and demands for governmental redress led by King were prophetic cries for justice, the multiethnic BLM demonstrations in varied parts of the United States after George Floyd's brutal murder were also examples of civil

reconciliation, as a close cousin (but not quite a sibling) of civil reconciliation in the 1960s.

Although the more recent resistance movement was not
directly associated with the church, it is grouped with civil reconciliation because the secular organizing around fairness and equity
is a spiritual descendant of the church's work during the civil rights
movement. Further, when ministers like Reverend Dr. William J.
Barber II, cochair of the Poor People's Campaign: A National Call
for Moral Revival, provide prophetic leadership in demanding governmental action on matters like increasing wages for poor and
low-income people and demanding police accountability for the
violence perpetuated against African Americans, the associated protest marches are popular examples of civil reconciliation.[30] Laws
like the Voting Rights Act and governmental policies like affirma-
tive action show how civil reconciliation leads to reparative justice,
an ethic that is clearly biblically based.

Conclusion

Within the context of the social construct called race, the reconciliation paradigm is rooted in a theology of equality, and
reparative justice must be a part of the reconciliation conversation. Although preaching is typically the way to open hearts
and minds and move them toward an alternative perspective,
prophetic leadership demands that clergy and laity alike understand the American dynamics of race, reconciliation, and repair.

The payment of "reparations" based on the federal government's previous actions should fall squarely within its province
as the entity both capable of paying them and culpable for the
injurious acts toward African Americans that necessitated them,
including the institution of slavery. Advocating for reparative justice requires that leaders understand the imbalances of the past to
promote healing today.

3

PROFILES IN PROPHETIC LEADERSHIP

Why have you despised the word of the Lord, to do what is evil in his sight? You have struck down Uriah the Hittite with the sword, and have taken his wife to be your wife, and have killed him with the sword of the Ammonites. Now therefore the sword shall never depart from your house, for you have despised me.

—2 Samuel 12:9–10

The hottest places in Hell are reserved for those who, in times of great moral crisis, maintain their neutrality.

—*Inferno* by Dante Alighieri (1265–1321)

First they came for the Socialists,
and I did not speak out—
Because I was not a Socialist.
Then they came for the Trade Unionists,
and I did not speak out—
Because I was not a Trade Unionist.
Then they came for the Jews, and I did not speak out—
Because I was not a Jew.
Then they came for me—and there
was no one left to speak for me.

—Martin Niemöller

Some say leadership cannot be taught and refer to others as "born leaders." Inasmuch as leadership is sometimes innate, in other instances, it is appropriately modeled. Consider the ministry of Jesus. In some way, shape, or form, aren't all Christians supposed to model their lives and leadership after Jesus?

The study of ecclesial leadership and the associated *munus triplex* doctrine use Christ as an exemplar while categorizing aspects of Jesus's leadership as falling into one or more of three different domains. Consequently, in the image of Christ, Christian leaders are often categorized as prophets, priests, or kings, with Christian leadership being prophetic, priestly, or royal. Just as Christianity is a learned faith tradition, Christian leadership can also be learned not only by studying Christ as the ultimate exemplar but by also studying other Christian leaders who have offered leadership in Christ's image. Two such leaders are Dietrich Bonhoeffer and Martin Luther King Jr.

The *munus triplex* doctrine looks at Christian leadership from both clergy and lay perspectives. While there are certainly biographical aspects of both Bonhoeffer and King—especially related to their early career services in pastoral ministry—that fit into the priestly and royal domains, the focus here is on them as *prophetic* leaders, highlighting the social circumstances that birthed the resistance-oriented leadership of both ministers.

Bonhoeffer and King are two of the church's most celebrated prophetic leaders and were also advocates for reconciliation in its three forms: *salvific, social,* and *civil.* Both ministers embraced salvific and social reconciliation because they advocated theologies of salvation *through* Jesus and for human equality *because of* Jesus. Both also publicly opposed governmental structures that did not embrace the equal treatment of all people. Indeed, King rejected Jim Crow segregation in America, and Bonhoeffer rejected the Nazi oppression of Jews in Third Reich Germany. Consequently, they were exemplars of all three aspects of reconciliation.

Theologies of atonement and eschatology that are often associated with salvific reconciliation are not the focus here. Rather, *social* and *civil* reconciliation are the focus areas because of the way they connect Scripture's social egalitarianism with prophetic resistance.

Connecting Social and Civil Reconciliation

As a natural outgrowth of social reconciliation, King and Bonhoeffer publicly spoke against the systems of injustice in their day. This type of prophetic leadership goes to the heart of civil reconciliation. Moreover, insofar as their public stances also evidenced a willingness to deal with the consequences of their actions, King and Bonhoeffer each had the prophetic courage to "speak truth to power" by addressing individuals and institutions with biblically grounded foundations for their prophetic resistance. The very concept of civil reconciliation—prophetically addressing governmental authorities or institutional systems of governance that oppress and subjugate marginalized groups—is a willingness to live out the moral imperative of human equality that is evidenced in Scripture's imperative for social reconciliation and at the heart of the overall reconciliation narrative.

Social Reconciliation and Empathy

Peter and Paul support social reconciliation: in Acts, Peter says that God shows no partiality of persons (Acts 10:34), and in 1 Corinthians, Paul says hierarchal social practices that make one class subservient to the other are abhorrent (1 Cor 11:17–22). The closely connected concept of civil reconciliation is a willingness to not only prophetically rebuke governing structures that are inconsistent with biblical teachings but also look introspectively at what happens if the church (*ekklesia*) fails in this moral imperative. Both Bonhoeffer and King believed the church was called to prophetic action and could not be silent in the face of injustice.

First, in exploring their willingness to literally speak truth to power, consider 2 Samuel 12:9–10. King David was both an individual and an institution in that under the monarchy, he also controlled all the Israelites' governmental power. Although David had God's favor, he wrongly mistreated Bathsheba's then spouse, Uriah, by deliberately and deceitfully sending him to the front lines of battle to die. David's egregiousness aggrieved God. By speaking up and in opposition to David, Nathan demonstrated the prophetic courage to tell Israel's head of state what "thus saith the Lord!" (2 Sam 12:7–11). Calling out establishment leaders is part of the prophetic leader's call.

Second, another part of the prophetic leader's call is empathy. The call is an empathic understanding of the potential consequences of what happens to society if leaders fail to address social injustices. For example, the third epigraph that begins this chapter is a famous quote by German theologian Martin Niemöller, head of Bonhoeffer's Confessing Church. The quote speaks to empathy. Embracing empathy means that prophetic leaders must be able to identify with others' social woes, although those woes may not be their own. One can think of example after example in America's sorted history of social hierarchy and ask, "What if no one spoke out on behalf of or in opposition to racism, sexism, classism, ageism, ableism, and so on?"

Empathy can be defined in terms of a cognitive awareness and an emotional response that corresponds to another's internal state.[1] A perfect illustration of this twofold definition is Bonhoeffer's ministry. Although Bonhoeffer was part of the "ruling class" in Germany's caste system, he truly learned about empathy from the Black church's freedom struggle during his yearlong engagement with Harlem's Abyssinian Baptist Church while studying under a postdoctoral Sloane Fellowship at Union Theological Seminary in New York. He came to understand sociopolitical oppression in ways he had not previously conceptualized. After understanding this type of systemic oppression, he had an emotional response. His heart was changed by his empathic understanding of Jewish oppression in Nazi Germany when he returned from America, and then he publicly *and prophetically* rejected Adolf Hitler's Third Reich.

The Prophetic Resistance of Civil Reconciliation

Because civil reconciliation deals with addressing governing authorities and structures, there must also be a willingness to accept the consequences of opposing the head of state. As a prophetic leader, Nathan literally spoke "truth to power" without an apparent concern of reprisal. His moral convictions led him to courageously address, head-on, an issue of how the state abused its powers in its treatment of another while he obviously could have drawn King David's ire and potential reprisal.

Daniel's famed story of the three Hebrew boys (Shadrach, Meshach, and Abednego) is an example of civil disobedience because the three boys became prophetic resistance leaders who were motivated by a selfless allegiance to God with a willingness to accept the consequences of speaking truth to or disagreeing with the head of state (Dan 3). Because they refused to comply with what they deemed to be an unjust and immoral law—one that demanded they bow down and swear allegiance to a statue of Nebuchadnezzar, the Babylonian king—the three Hebrew boys fearlessly opted instead for prophetic resistance, fully aware that they would be punished and sent into a fiery furnace. King even cites the three Hebrew boys as an example of the moral mandate to stand up to injustice without fear of reprisal in his famous "Letter from Birmingham City Jail," which he wrote while incarcerated over Easter weekend in 1963 because of his own prophetic resistance.[2]

With Bonhoeffer, this same prophetic resistance and acceptance of unmerited suffering became a core part of his theology after returning to Germany in 1931. After experiencing empathy for those in Harlem and then publicly rejecting Hitler, Bonhoeffer wrote *The Cost of Discipleship* in 1937.

Bonhoeffer addresses the prophetic nature of suffering being redemptive: "If they are content to not pitch their hopes too high, they will not be perturbed when Jesus warns them that their way among men will be one of suffering. But there is a miraculous power latent in this suffering. Whereas the criminal has to suffer his punishment in secret, the disciples will have to stand before governors and kings 'for my sake'. . . . This suffering will help forward their testimony. It is part of God's plan and the will of Jesus."[3] For Bonhoeffer, this meant that despite their fear and expectation of suffering, German Christians had a moral responsibility to speak out for their Jewish brothers and sisters who were being subjugated by the Nazi political regime.

Racial and Ethnic Discrimination in the United States and Germany

Racism and anti-Semitism are closely related in that both are forms of prejudice and evil. Under both oppressive systems, a subservient class is dehumanized by a dominant class. The subjugation of Blacks in the United States and of Jews in Nazi Germany represent examples of racism and ethnic cleansing, two evils with a long and sorted history.

In the United States, both the legalized institution of slavery and its post-emancipation system of Jim Crow segregation scarred and *continue to scar* both Blacks and whites. *Race* is nothing more than a social construct whereby various peoples are classified based on immutable characteristics. In its most practical terms, "race is an evolving social idea that was created to legitimize racial inequality and protect white advantage."[4] I have often given presentations and illustrated the social construction of race by noting that people perceive me as a *Black* man. My follow-up rhetorical question is often, "Why wouldn't you call me a *blue* man?" (Blue is my favorite color, and I often wear blue suits.) The reason is that society has associated the term *Black* with people who have physical characteristics like mine: characteristics that are the opposite of "white."

Similarly, society has associated the descriptive term *white* with people who possess another set of immutable characteristics, those shared by the dominant class that controlled the tripartite socioeconomic engine of genocide, enslavement, and colonization that led to the establishment of the United States. It's a historical fact that the term *white* first appeared in colonial law in the late 1600s, setting a socialized foundation for the 1790 census, when people originally claimed their race. It was then—from the 1800s through the early twentieth century, as more and more immigrants entered the United States—that the concept of race as we perceive it today was solidified.[5]

Further, after the adoption of the Thirteenth Amendment in 1865 and the abolishment of slavery in the United States, "whiteness" remained profoundly important because, as legalized racism and violence against African Americans continued to manifest in new ways, "to have citizenship—and the rights citizenship imbued—you had to be legally classified as white."[6] In other words, the phenomenon known as *race* in America was something humans constructed for socioeconomic justification.

In going a step further, the inherent value humans have historically placed and continue to place on people within various racially identified groups goes to the core of the associated system known as *racism* in America. Indeed, through each period of American history, the country has struggled—*and continues to struggle*—with the issue of race. As Eddie S. Glaude Jr. argues in *Democracy in Black: How Race Still Enslaves the American Soul*, the lofty ideal expressed in the Declaration of Independence that "all men are created equal" has been met with the reality that some men and women are valued as less than others because of the color of their skin.[7] This is a value gap that has consistently been associated with race in America.

In addition to racism, anti-Semitism has been a dehumanizing evil that has followed Christianity since its inception, with a prejudice rooted in ethnicity. My usage of the term *ethnic* comes from the Greek word *ethnikon*, which means "foreign" or "national," and relates to communities with common religious or cultural traits. To illustrate the difference between race and ethnicity, consider both the similarities and the differences between whites and Jews in Nazi Germany. At face value, both groups shared common *racial* characteristics. Jews, however, shared certain distinct cultural and religious traits. Hitler's Nazi Germany did not create anti-Semitism. As the Genesis narrative portrays, the Hebrews' enslavement in Egypt was based on their ethnicity. In Jesus's day, he was an oppressed ethnic minority living under the Roman Empire's caste system. Hitler merely used an already existing anti-Semitism, a form of *ethnic* discrimination, that had been ingrained in society almost since the beginning of time.

The same can be said of the United States, especially as it relates to the social construct of race and the consequential *racist* treatment of Blacks. Indeed, a similar vein of racism in America has so significantly influenced the country's sociopolitical existence. For example, in *White Evangelical Racism*, Anthea Butler describes the former social conditions and the origins of the very polarized white evangelicalism of today, especially the developing religion of the Lost Cause that attempted to justify racial subjugation in the South.

Butler shows how evangelicalism replaced slavery as the South's cohesive narrative by writing, "It also maintained the most important element of slavery: the idea that Black people were inferior to whites and therefore unable to take an equal place economically or socially in the Reconstruction South."[8] This is why so many white supremacists, especially those associated with the church, romanticized the religion of a Lost Cause as a form of civil religion rooted in white nationalism, as they refused and continue to refuse to accept Blacks as equals.[9] Indeed, many white evangelicals and Christian nationalists were the staunchest supporters of the regressive voter suppression laws that were specifically targeted at Blacks in 2021. A closer analysis of Bonhoeffer and King reveals why the church's prophetic leaders must embrace empathy and address the two evils of ethnic and racial discrimination.

Bonhoeffer and the Black Church

Although Bonhoeffer was from Germany, he gained an empathic insight into the issue of ethnic discrimination in Germany through the racism he witnessed in America. He was also deeply influenced by the Black church's social justice–oriented work toward eradicating racism.

While at Union, Bonhoeffer began to reject the secularization of Christianity, along with the ethical and social idealism he saw as so prevalent in progressive white churches. Bonhoeffer became close friends with four Union students who all had very different backgrounds: Jean Lasserre was French, Erwin Sutz was Swiss, Paul Lehmann was American, and Albert Franklin Fisher was Black. While Bonhoeffer's experiences with each of them formed him, his closeness with Frazier, a minister from Alabama and Howard University graduate, most deeply shaped his life and future as a prophetic leader.

When Fisher invited Bonhoeffer to Harlem's Abyssinian Baptist Church, Bonhoeffer readily went along, not realizing that while there, in the African American community, he would empathically experience the ethic of suffering. Reggie L. Williams addresses this ethic in *Bonhoeffer's Black Jesus: Harlem Renaissance Theology and an Ethic of Resistance* when he writes, "Jesus was evidence that God knows suffering; if God was with Jesus in his suffering at the hands of injustice, then surely God is with black people who suffer in America."[10]

Bonhoeffer was heavily formed by the prophetic leadership of Reverend Adam Clayton Powell Sr., Abyssinian's senior pastor. In *Bonhoeffer: Pastor, Martyr, Prophet, Spy*, Eric Metaxas describes Reverend Powell's unabashed prophetic leadership and the influence it had on Bonhoeffer by writing, "He [Powell] was active in combating racism and minced no words about the saving power of Jesus Christ. He didn't fall for the Hobson's choice of one or the other; he believed that without both, one had neither, but with both, one had everything and more. When the two were combined, *and only then*, God came into the equation. . . . For the first time, Bonhoeffer saw the gospel preached and lived out in obedience to God's commands. He was entirely captivated and, for the rest of his time in New York, he was there every Sunday to worship."[11] Stated otherwise, Powell was living out the church's prophetic witness in such a way that Bonhoeffer's life was changed by a new understanding of the gospel. Bonhoeffer then articulated a worldview of the two planes of the Christian cross: the vertical representing the church's salvific role and its work for the kingdom to come and the horizontal representing the church's social justice agenda and its work in the kingdom at hand.

Bonhoeffer embraced this understanding as he returned to Germany, speaking truth to power and rejecting the Nazi government's systemic oppression of Jews. Just like the Daniel 3 narrative of the three Hebrew boys, Bonhoeffer was not afraid to lose his life for his moral beliefs. Indeed, in *The Cost of Discipleship*, Bonhoeffer speaks to this ethic, famously drawing a contrast between *cheap* and *costly* grace by writing, "It is costly because it costs a man his life, and it is grace because it gives a man the only true life."[12] This ethic speaks to a core tenant of Bonhoeffer's prophetic leadership.

Another one of Bonhoeffer's friends at Union, the French pacifist Jean Lasserre, helped form Bonhoeffer's devotion to a nonviolent prophetic resistance to evil. Bonhoeffer took that passion for peace into his ecumenical work and was a different person when he left America in 1931. He cared about international relations in Germany and the poor living in the slums. He was fully committed to his faith; he was "the theologian who had become a Christian."[13] It was therefore Bonhoeffer's Christ-centered and empathic embrace of others that manifested through both prophetic activism *and* peaceful resistance when he returned to Germany.

Bonhoeffer and Prophetic Leadership

To fully appreciate Bonhoeffer's transformation in New York and his coming to embrace the redemptive suffering of Christianity as part of the liberating gospel of Jesus, his background in Germany shows that he was, to paraphrase the famed Howard Thurman, a theologian "in head" who ultimately became a Christian "in heart." Bonhoeffer's empathic commitment to the gospel of Jesus, especially the Sermon on the Mount, became a focal point of his ministry in Nazi Germany and one of the reasons he so passionately identified with his socially marginalized Jewish brothers and sisters.

Further, like Bonhoeffer, King's gravitation to prophetic leadership was also the result of social exposure. The difference, however, was that whereas Bonhoeffer empathically *embraced* the marginalized "Other," King *was* the marginalized "Other," in that he was a member of the marginalized class he spoke out to represent. As an African American from the South, King personally knew the immoral harm done by Jim Crow segregation. Moreover, as the son of a prominent minister, he was also socially influenced by his father's contemporaries, including those who led in the Black church's prophetic resistance movement. Stated otherwise, King's social exposure formed him to be a prophetic leader too.

Bonhoeffer's Background

Dietrich was born to his parents, Karl and Paula, on February 4, 1906, approximately ten minutes before his twin sister, Sabine. He was one of eight children, the fourth and youngest son. All the Bonhoeffer children were born in Breslau, where their father was chair of the psychiatry and neurology departments at the local university and director of the University of Breslau Wroclaw Mental Hospital, an institution for nervous diseases.

When Bonhoeffer was six, his family moved to Berlin because his father accepted an appointment to be chair of psychology and neurology. As a medical doctor and scientist, moving to Berlin made Karl Bonhoeffer head of his field in Germany. It also put him at occasional intellectual odds with other leaders in his field, including Sigmund Freud, Carl Jung, and Alfred Adler. Karl Bonhoeffer was somewhat agnostic because of his views on psychoanalysis and religion and was biased against matters not associated with analytical reason. Paula Bonhoeffer, however, was religious.

When Bonhoeffer and his twin sister were just eight years old, in 1914, war broke out. By 1917, the Bonhoeffer family personally felt its tragic effects when the oldest boys, Karl-Friedrich and Walter, were called up for military service. By April 1918, Walter was mobilized, and two weeks later, he was killed. His death was a turning point for Bonhoeffer in his transformation from childhood. In 1920, at the age of thirteen and while enrolled in an elite school in Berlin, Bonhoeffer surprised his parents when he shared that he wanted to become a theologian. This was a bold move considering the dynamics of Bonhoeffer's household. He knew his father would be polite, but he also knew his father would disagree with his chosen vocation.

Four years later, after following a family tradition and studying for a year at Tubingen, Bonhoeffer had a revelation that influenced his vocational thinking. While visiting Rome, he came to conceptualize the church as much more than his Lutheran Protestant Church of Germany. Instead, he began conceptualizing a universal Christian community. *What was the church?* This question became the central focus of Bonhoeffer's doctoral and post-doctoral writing as well as his subsequent ecumenical work in Europe.

After returning from Rome, in June 1924, Bonhoeffer transferred from Tubingen and enrolled at Berlin University. As a theology candidate, he was also required to engage in parish ministry. Although he could have sought waivers from his professors, Bonhoeffer did the opposite. He was deeply engaged in leading a Sunday school class at the Grunewald Parish Church. He earned his doctorate at the end of 1927 at the age of twenty-one. By this time, something changed in Bonhoeffer's family that would profoundly influence his personal perception of Hitler's Nazi Germany in the years to come, especially in the years after he returned from America. His twin sister, Sabine, got engaged to a young Jewish lawyer, Gerhard Leibholz.

In February 1928, Bonhoeffer left Berlin for Barcelona to serve a one-year term as the assistant to Pastor Friedrich Olbricht. During his tenure, Bonhoeffer preached nineteen sermons when Pastor Olbricht was traveling and led the children's church. Parish ministry in Barcelona was also Bonhoeffer's first serious encounter with poverty, as he began a ministry to help the unemployed. The experience helped develop his preaching. Although asked to remain in Barcelona, Bonhoeffer also wanted to complete his post-doctoral work. He returned to Berlin in February 1929.

Bonhoeffer was in somewhat of a quagmire. He enjoyed parish ministry in Barcelona so much that he pondered leaving academia. At twenty-three, however, he had not yet reached the requisite age of twenty-five to be ordained as a Lutheran pastor. Since he didn't want to close the possibility of a career in academia, he did a postdoctoral thesis, "Act and Being," where he again wrestled with the question, "What is the church?" He completed his work in February 1930, was examined on July 8, and gave his first university lecture on July 31. Still wrestling with wanting to become a pastor, because of a Sloane Fellowship at Union Theological Seminary, by the fall of that same year, Bonhoeffer was headed to New York. It was there that the "theologian" truly came to experience Christ in an intimate and personal way and began to develop into a prophetic leader!

Bonhoeffer's Black Jesus in America and Germany

Just as Bonhoeffer was deeply engaged in parish life during his studies in Berlin, he was deeply engaged in the teaching ministry at Abyssinian Baptist Church in Harlem. Through his connection with Albert Franklin Fisher and his exposure to Black Harlem, Bonhoeffer was motivated because he learned what it meant to have meaningful Christianity.

In *Bonhoeffer's Black Jesus: Harlem Renaissance Theology and an Ethic of Resistance*, Reggie L. Williams writes, "Experiences of spiritual growth in Harlem gave Bonhoeffer a healthier encounter with Jesus by way of a connection between Jesus and suffering within an ethic of resistance that identifies Jesus with the oppressed, rather than the oppressors."[14] Because of this key formation, he equated Black suffering in America with Jesus's suffering for all of humanity. This revelation allowed him to see German Christianity's distortions and to counter them with prophetic resistance. After experiencing the Black Christ in America and returning to Germany in 1931, Bonhoeffer had a new understanding of Christianity.

After returning to Germany, he spent significant time with Karl Barth, who was teaching at the university in Bonn. Before his November 15 ordination, Bonhoeffer wrote a Lutheran catechism based on Acts 17:26 ("From one ancestor he made all nations to inhabit the whole earth, and he allotted the times of their existence and the boundaries of the places where they would live"). He warned about the sin of the *Volk* theology of racial purity in Germany, as it nationalized a belief that all "Other" people were inferior. But his Black Christ–influenced theology now espoused a belief that *all* humans came from one blood. His catechism supports the belief that "the sin of racism is just cause for Christians to oppose the state if necessary, in concrete obedience to Christ's commandment to love one's neighbor."[15] Bonhoeffer's new perspectives, especially in turbulent Germany, placed him at significant variance with his colleagues in both the academy and the pulpit.

After his time with Barth and subsequent ordination, Bonhoeffer joined the faculty at the University of Berlin as a lecturer and became a chaplain to the students at a technical college in Charlottenburg. This period between 1931 and 1933 proved difficult for Bonhoeffer because of Nazism's rising influence on both students and faculty alike. His frustrations with the German church also sharpened his theological focus.

Bonhoeffer's desire to serve the poor and marginalized led him to leave Germany once again. From 1933 to 1935, he served as the pastor of two German congregations in London and returned to the University of Berlin in the fall of 1935. Bonhoeffer had a combined role as a subversive director of the Confessing Church Seminary at Finkenwalde, an *illegal seminary* where he openly trained pastors who opposed the Nazification of the German state church. This put him at odds with the University of Berlin, and his teaching credentials were revoked in 1936. In many regards, this was the beginning of the end.

Bonhoeffer's empathy caused him to grow in his resistance as a prophetic leader in the Confessing Church. The Nazis had cracked down on the church, arresting more than eight hundred pastors in 1937 alone, the same year Bonhoeffer released *The Cost of Discipleship*. In late June, the Confessing Church's leader, Martin Niemöller, preached what we would call a "prophetic sermon" by speaking truth against the Nazi institution of power. He was arrested days later and remained incarcerated until rescued by the Allies in 1945. Moreover, in 1938, Hitler's conflated church/state presented an ultimatum for the Confessing Church. Just as the three Hebrew boys were faced with an ultimatum of either bowing down to worship a statue of King Nebuchadnezzar or facing mortal penalty (Dan 3), pastors were being forced to swear personal allegiance to Hitler. When it seemed like matters couldn't get any worse, Bonhoeffer experienced *Kristallnacht* (the night of broken glass; November 9, 1938), when anti-Semitic Nazis stormed Jewish homes and businesses as well as synagogues, destroying property and killing Jewish people.

In the wake of this massacre, Bonhoeffer meditated on these words: "They burned all the meeting places of God in the land" (Ps 74:8), connecting them with other passages of Scripture to rebuke Germany's anti-Semitic claim that Jews were cursed because they had not accepted Christ. By specifically identifying with the evil being done to Jews and taking a scripturally based position to oppose it, "Bonhoeffer was using the words of Jews— David, Zechariah, and Paul—to make the point that the Jews are God's people. . . . He had never abandoned them."[16] The following year, in 1939, as Bonhoeffer was deeply conflicted about the nationalization of Germany's Reich Church, he also received notice of his potential call-up for military service.

Bonhoeffer went back to New York for only twenty-six days after accepting and then declining an opportunity to teach at Union and serve as a pastor to German refugees in New York. Ultimately, he reversed his decision to return to America because he believed it was a mistake. With World War II imminent, Bonhoeffer concluded that if he did not live with his people in Germany through the war years, he would be of no service to them during the country's reconstruction.[17] After war broke out, Bonhoeffer became a member of the Abwehr, a German military intelligence agency that was at the center of resistance to Hitler.

On August 9, 1945—just two weeks before the Allied forces liberated Flossenbürg, the last of four prisons to detain Bonhoeffer during his two years of incarceration—he was killed by Nazi forces. Martyred at thirty-nine, he lived fourteen years as a changed man, after his encounter with the Black Christ of suffering. As a pastor, some of his service was in *priestly* leadership. Other service was undoubtedly in *royal* leadership. But his empathic embrace of Jews who were oppressed by Hitler's anti-Semitic Nazi regime and ethnically marginalized by Germany's caste system grounded him in a resistance movement that was rooted in the *prophetic* leadership domain. Bonhoeffer ultimately gave his life in furtherance of a moral cause in which he deeply believed.

King's Social Exposure

King grew up in the South as a true son of the church and a product of the Black church experience. In addition to his father being a prominent minister, his grandfather and great-grandfather were ministers too. Initially, his desire *was not* to serve in ordained ministry. He originally desired to become either a lawyer or a medical doctor to address many of the systemic social inequities he saw between Blacks and whites in American life. He also had a disdain for the excessive histrionics he often saw in African American preaching. Contemporary students of homiletics learn that a good sermon should touch congregants with *logos* (logic), *ethos* (character or credibility of the speaker), and *pathos* (emotion). King observed that because so many Black ministers of his youth lacked theological resources and formalized academic training, they often had an imbalanced reliance on *pathos*. He had no intention to become a "typical" Black preacher.

The Academic and Practical Intersection
of King's Developing Theology

During his undergraduate studies at Morehouse College, King was mentored by his father's close friend Benjamin Mays, who served as Morehouse's president. He developed a different view of ministry. He tremendously benefited from his teachers' combined emphasis on deep Christian faith *and* analytical thought. By King's senior year at Morehouse, he too wanted to become a preacher.

While studying at Crozer Seminary, from 1948 to 1951, King was mentored by one of his father's friends, J. Pius Barbour, the politically progressive and legendary pastor of Calvary Baptist Church in Chester, Pennsylvania. It was also during his time at Crozer that King began a deep theological quest for a methodology to eliminate social evils. In addition to studying philosophical and ethical thought leaders in social Christianity, like Walter Rauschenbusch, King also studied Greek philosophers and developed a dialectal manner of reasoning influenced by the German philosopher Georg Wilhelm Friedrich Hegel.

After returning from a trip to India, where King personally experienced the life and teachings of Mohandas Gandhi, he heard Howard University president Mordecai Johnson deliver a sermon at Philadelphia's Fellowship House. Johnson's preaching sparked in King an intense desire to deeply study Gandhi and his methods of nonviolent resistance during India's independence movement. This transitioning experience helped form the King America was introduced to when he led a prophetic ministry of nonviolent resistance at the onset of the Montgomery bus boycott just a few years later in 1955. In 1951, however, as King began his doctoral studies at Boston University, he was also mentored by two of his father's friends: William H. Hester, pastor of Boston's historic Twelfth Baptist Church, and Howard Thurman, the university's first Black dean of the chapel.

At Boston, King refined his theology and made critical decisions that would affect not only his future but the entire United States. He decided against a career in academia, opting instead to pursue pastoral ministry and accepting the offer to serve Dexter Avenue Baptist Church in Montgomery, Alabama. He also began dating Coretta Scott (a fellow southerner who was originally from Marion, Alabama) while she was studying at the New England Conservatory. They were married on June 18, 1953.

Almost a year after his wedding, in May 1954—the same time the Supreme Court decided the landmark case *Brown v. Board of Education*—King earned his doctorate. Shortly thereafter, on September 1, he became the full-time pastor of Dexter Avenue Baptist Church, just more than a year before the civil rights movement officially began, with Rosa Parks's civil disobedience and King's prophetic leadership in shaping the successful Montgomery bus boycott. As the old expression goes, "The rest is history."

Conclusion

Social circumstances create prophetic leaders. In the case of King, a son of the South, the social circumstances of Jim Crow segregation compelled him to accept the call to prophetic leadership instead of a career in academia. Moreover, as a member of a marginalized class, social circumstances also created King's prophetic witness, just as they did in the cases of oppressed biblical figures like the three Hebrew boys (Shadrach, Meshach, and Abednego) and in the case of the ultimate prophetic leadership exemplar, Jesus the Christ.

Likewise, the same can be said of Bonhoeffer, with the exception that he *was not* a member of a marginalized class. In Bonhoeffer's case, the circumstances that created his prophetic leadership included an empathic understanding of the social harm done by discrimination. In prophetically proclaiming the need for fairness and justice while simultaneously breaking ties with *the oppressor* and identifying with the suffering of *the oppressed*, empathy motivated Bonhoeffer's prophetic witness. With the voice of a prophet, Bonhoeffer chose the side of the oppressed.

Having explored how social circumstances have called and created prophetic leaders in the past, we will now look at how social circumstances are again calling prophetic leaders today, by looking at the cultural framework of Christian nationalism and America's ongoing immigration crisis—social justice issues the church simply cannot ignore.

SOCIAL INJUSTICES THE CHURCH CANNOT IGNORE

When an alien resides with you in your land, you shall not
oppress the alien. The alien who resides with you shall be
to you as the citizen among you; you shall love the alien
as yourself, for you were aliens in the land of Egypt.

—Leviticus 19:33–34

Martin Luther King Jr. and Dietrich Bonhoeffer are clergy exemplars who led in the prophetic domain of ministry. While following their respective moral compasses, faith compelled them to take positions that were responsive to the social conditions of their time. Insofar as they were examples of prophetic leadership during *their time*, the question is now whether contemporary church leaders are prepared to respond to social conditions during *this time*. There are many relevant social injustice issues that the contemporary American church must address, such as immigration reform. If the American church is to provide leadership in the present age, its leaders cannot be silent about this issue, among many others.

Beginning with a scriptural overview of immigration that views migrants as our siblings in Christ, as opposed to "Others" with whom we can neither identify nor build community, church leaders must engage in the resistance politics of a renewed Sanctuary Movement by responding to America's ongoing immigration crisis with calls for reform. Church leaders must prophetically reject the tribalism of the "Make America Great Again" (#MAGA) political narrative—along with its companion, the cultural framework of Christian nationalism that rejects, vilifies, and castigates migrants as "less than"—citing King's prophetic leadership as an exemplar of how the church should respond when human-made and divine laws do not comport with one another.[1]

By invoking the #MAGA political narrative, the reference is *not* limited to a particular politician or political candidacy. Instead, it is a mindset that is emblematic of America's most divisive and darkest days. There are some factions that believe the church should not be involved in secular politics. There are also other factions that have conflated Christianity and patriotism to create a Christian nationalism and theocratic allegiance to a partisan political party, as opposed to a divine allegiance to Jesus the Christ. Both factions are wrong and must be called out by prophetic leaders through the practice of prophetic preaching.

In specifically calling out the #MAGA narrative to illustrate the importance of prophetic preaching, O. Wesley Allen Jr. writes in *Preaching in the Era of Trump*, "Preachers are called to be prophets who address, indeed counter the kinds of oppressive intentions Trump has expressed during his campaign. We cannot claim to serve a God of justice and be silent about such things in the pulpit."[2] Stated otherwise, the gospel teaches us equality in the name of Jesus (Gal 3:28). Prophetic preaching calls on us to share the good news of human equality with others.

In response to the social injustice often associated with America's religious factions, prophetic preaching calls out those injustices and the policies behind them. Someone must address the wrongful immigration policies and ideas about immigrants that were put in place by the #MAGA political narrative. The immigration policies may be the "laws of the land," but they conflict with the moral "laws of God." They have fueled *and continue to fuel* the weekly sermons of many politically progressive preachers, including yours truly. In connecting the Christian faith with a prophetic resistance for social justice, in the image of Jesus, I urge the American church to adopt a theology of welcome that is rooted in Scripture.

As it relates to immigration reform, in a theology of welcome, as opposed to the "open borders" policy, the American church should do at least two things: (1) recognize the crisis our current policies continue to present and (2) urge the US government to address meaningful immigration reform. Large numbers of faith-based organizations—including Catholic Charities USA, the Episcopal Church, the Lutheran Immigration and Refugee Service, the stated clerk of the Presbyterian Church (USA), the US Conference of Catholic Bishops, and the General Board of Church and Society of the United Methodist Church, along with the Wider Church Ministries of the United Church of Christ—all joined together in supporting comprehensive immigration reform.[3] Until Congress acts, however, pursuant to its plenary power as defined within the Constitution, the American church's prophetic leaders should be guided by Scripture and must speak out in providing the resistance needed to light a proverbial fire and prod the government to move past partisan bickering and into positive action. Indeed, immigration is one of the most significant and public-facing social justice issues of the current day.

A Biblical Perspective on Immigration

Immigration is a tool God repeatedly uses to unite people of different races and ethnicities, allowing them to discover commonality and community while moving past previously held presumptions. This perspective provides the framework for a theology of welcome that includes understanding immigration and embracing policies that support immigrants while simultaneously rejecting the polarizing politics of Christian nationalism that often invoke the negative animus of "us" versus "them" instead of recognizing that God's children have roots in different parts of the human diaspora.

Mainline Christian denominations have historically expressed an openness to the immigration of people from other countries and a willingness to help them succeed in the United States.[4] In the American context, such "strangers" or immigrants are typically classified as people who are from another country but are living in the United States, documented or undocumented. Indeed, most foreign-born people living in the United States do have legal status. All immigrants do not. In *Welcoming the Stranger*, Matthew Soerens and Jenny Yang write, "Of an estimated 44.7 million people born outside but living inside the United States, about twenty million are already naturalized US citizens, and roughly twelve million are Lawful Permanent Residents. . . . Most foreign-born individuals—about three out of four—are present lawfully."[5] The remainder of immigrants—approximately eleven million people—do not have legal status. In looking deeper than overly broad categorizations of either "legal" or "illegal," all humans are God's children; everyone deserves humane treatment.

Migration in the Old Testament

There are several Hebrew words for "immigrant" that have been translated into English. They include *alien*, *stranger*, *sojourner*, and *foreigner*, depending on the translation. Like immigrants today, the protagonists of the Old Testament left their homelands and migrated to other lands for a variety of reasons. In Genesis 11, for example, *Abram*, later *Abraham*, is introduced as an immigrant (11:31). Faith motivated him to migrate to Canaan with his family, such that he would fulfill his divine destiny (12:1–9). Indeed, his decision to leave Ur and bring his family to Canaan parallels the stories of many immigrants who leave their homelands to cross borders because they too feel compelled to lead better lives. Even

Abraham's detention in and deportation from Egypt (12:10–20) is strikingly like the stories of so many Latinx and Haitian migrants who have been detained and/or deported under US policies.

The Genesis 18 narrative also shows Abraham as an exemplar of hospitality to foreigners. When three strangers arrived at his home, little did he know they were messengers from God. He was simply eager to be hospitable. Consider the following scriptural passage:

> The Lord appeared to Abraham by the oaks of Mamre, as he sat at the entrance of his tent in the heart of the day. He looked up and saw three men standing near him. When he saw them, he ran from the tent entrance to meet them, and bowed down to the ground. He said, "My lord, if I find favor with you, do not pass by your servant. Let a little water be brought, and wash your feet, and rest yourselves under the tree. Let me bring a little bread, that you may refresh yourselves, and after that you may pass on—since you have come to your servant." So they said, "Do as you have said." And Abraham hastened into the tent to Sarah, and said, "Make ready quickly three measures of choice flour, knead it, and make cakes." Abraham ran to the herd, and took a calf, tender and good, and gave it to the servant, who hastened to prepare it. Then he took curds and milk and the calf that he had prepared, and sent it before them; and he stood by them under the tree while they ate. (Gen 18:1–9)

Abraham's welcome was no doubt the consequence of his own experiences as an immigrant in a foreign land. This is arguably like modern-day immigrants to the United States being embraced by those who came before them in helping acclimate and orient new immigrants to American culture.

Not all Old Testament immigrants are *from* Israel. There is also migration *into* Israel. In the book of Ruth, the narrative's namesake is a woman from Moab who marries a foreigner in her home country. After her foreign husband's death, however, Ruth decides to follow her mother-in-law, Naomi, to the foreign land of Judah, even after being sternly cautioned to do otherwise (Ruth 1:15–18). Her clear determination embodies the spirit of so many contemporary immigrants who also leave their homelands for the sake of family. Unfortunately, there are countless immigrants detained at the US/Mexico border who have been separated from their loved ones, including numerous children.[6]

In Exodus, God uses Moses to lead the Israelites from an oppressive dictatorial governmental rule in Egypt, essentially as immigrants who were promised the eventual habitation of the land of Canaan (Exod 3:7–8). Consequently, under Moses's leadership, the Israelites became refugees who fled Egyptian persecution by escaping under God's divine direction to find a new land. In doing so, like so many refugees today, they also found significant challenges.[7] If the church remains true to its biblically based values, prophetic leadership demands that its current leaders—modern-day versions of Moses—be more outspoken in demanding governmental reform on immigration policies.

Migration in the New Testament

In the New Testament, the most popular contextualized example of immigration is the birth and ministry of Jesus, as Matthew records Mary and Joseph fleeing with their infant child to Egypt, fearing King Herod would kill them if they remained in Bethlehem of Judea (Matt 2:13). Indeed, this narrative of Jesus as an immigrant refugee directly parallels the stories of so many families who flee dictatorial rule or persecution in their native lands too.

Although the New Testament speaks less expressly about immigrants than the Old Testament, there is an implied reference to immigration in Hebrews when the author advises readers to welcome strangers with hospitality because, in doing so, one may be entertaining angels without knowing it (Heb 13:2). The book of Acts also notes how God used migration to spread the gospel. When Stephen was martyred, "a severe persecution began against the church in Jerusalem, and *all* except the apostles were scattered throughout the countryside of Judea and Samaria" (Acts 8:1; emphasis added). God used the dispersion of Jesus's followers to spread the gospel throughout Judea and beyond. Phillip, for example, went south toward Gaza and shared the gospel with an Ethiopian pilgrim who accepted the good news and presumably brought it back to Africa. God has indeed used migration to bring disparate groups into communion with one another.

As a pastor in a Black church tradition, with a history of active prophetic leadership, I urge members of the church universal, both clergy *and* lay, to embrace immigration from the scriptural perspective of God using it and its associated human migration to place different peoples in association with one another and foster diversity among all peoples. Members of the church should receive God's divine intention and embrace a theology of welcome for "the Other" based on the equality of all humans.

The Lesson of Migration in Scripture

In considering the foregoing scriptural examples, from both the Old and New Testaments, it is evident that God deliberately uses migration—a process of causing people who had been isolated in ethnically homogeneous communities to move into newly formed multiethnic social settings—to place different peoples in social community with the Other. The causes for such moves will not always be comfortable. God has God's way of making us move, in God's own perfect timing. Indeed, if there is any takeaway from these scriptural narratives on migration, we must see migration as a tool God repeatedly uses to unite people of different ethnicities, allowing them to discover commonality and community while simultaneously moving past previous presumptions.

The #MAGA Practice of (Un)welcome

Some people deliberately advocate policy positions of "unwelcome" because they play into politically popular prejudices. The 2016 presidential campaign of Donald Trump and his "Make America Great Again" rhetoric vilified Mexicans as "rapists and murders," and the Trump administration subsequently separated migrant children from their families—all examples of reasons why the church must "get political" and do so through its advocacy in prophetic preaching.

Trump's campaign promised to build a border wall to prevent (illegal) immigration and ultimately stop the continued growth of the United States' immigrant population, which spoke to the worst impulses of a specific American demographic that longed for a return to the "white rule" of yesteryear. Indeed, such rhetoric emboldens those white nationalists who embrace the so-called replacement theory, a fear that immigrants, minorities, and Jews are replacing white Protestants in America's social hierarchy. With a foundation supported by beliefs in the United States' "manifest destiny," such language of *unwelcome* goes hand in hand with the rise of white Christian nationalism in the United States.

Prejudicial attitudes toward immigrants were inflamed by Trump's border wall language as part of the 2016 presidential campaign. While addressing various aspects of Christian nationalism—particularly how it typecasts the "Other" as being outside of the established cultural framework of America—because support for Christian nationalism favors boundaries, *especially national boundaries*, it breeds xenophobia: "As Americans more closely connect Christian identity with America civil belonging, they become more likely to believe that immigrants undermine American culture and increase crime rates. Unsurprisingly, they are also all the more eager to reduce immigration into the United States."[8] This is the specific demographic to which Trump's 2016 campaign rhetoric spoke. This #MAGA mindset—not limited to Trump or any specific political campaign—must be addressed through prophetic preaching throughout the American church.

Indeed, some Christians are against discussing social justice in the church at all. Glenn Beck, a former FOX News host, made a comment that became a litmus test for some conservative evangelical Christians: "I beg you, look for the words 'social justice' or 'economic justice' on your church website, if you find it, run as fast as you can. Social justice and economic justice, they are code words"—terms he believes indicate communism or Nazism. He also said, "If you have a priest that is pushing social justice, go find another parish. Go alert your bishop."[9]

In *Jesus and John Wayne*, a book connecting the rise of a hypermasculine, white American patriarchy with evangelical Christianity and the #MAGA political narrative, Kristin Kobes Du Mez writes, "White evangelicals are more opposed to immigration reform and have more negative views of immigrants than any other religious demographic; two-thirds support[ed] Trump's border wall."[10] With respect to evangelicals, Christian nationalism—a belief that America is God's chosen nation and must be defended as such—serves as a powerful predictor of intolerance toward immigrants.[11] Just like there is a clear division in society at large as to how immigration should be viewed, there is a similar tension in the ways various factions within the church embrace the ministry of social justice and associated immigration policies.

In August 2019, immigration authorities within the Trump administration raided seven food processing plants in small towns outside Jackson, Mississippi, leading to the arrests of 680 mostly Latino workers. Jackson's mayor, Chokwe Antar Lumumba, called on his city's churches and faith communities to provide sanctuary for immigrant neighbors.[12] This was not the first time he defied the Trump administration on the issue of immigration. In 2017, former attorney general Jeff Sessions referred to Jackson and twenty-eight other localities as "sanctuary cities," a reference to "sanctuary" as a place of refuge for immigrants that began in the 1980s Sanctuary Movement. Sessions referenced those respective cities because they offered protection to so many undocumented immigrants. Sessions threatened Jackson and other such cities with losing eligibility to seek some $4.1 billion available in federal grant funding.[13]

The August 2019 raids were not the Trump administration's first controversial acts related to immigration. During the administration's first year, in September 2017, it also announced its intent to wind down the Deferred Action for Childhood Arrivals Program. Indeed, considering that the longest government shutdown in American history resulted from Trump's demand for $5.7 billion to build a US/Mexico border wall, it is safe to say that the administration's position on immigration was one of its most controversial.[14]

Revisiting Immigrant Classifications: Considerations of Theological Discernment

The ultimate authority for Christians on any topic ought to be the Bible. For many evangelical Christians, however, "refugees" and "immigration" are *political* issues rather than biblically based moral concerns.[15] Perhaps this disconnect is because immigration is not typically discussed in church (let alone from the pulpit) and is consequently seen as "separate" from our lives, except for national news or political debates. In *Discerning Welcome*, however, Ellen Clark Clémot makes immigration reform a matter of congregational concern (one of the goals of prophetic preaching) while also prophetically advocating for a political theology of discernment that supports welcoming refugees as neighbors.[16]

There are many nuances of immigrant classifications, whereby (illegal) immigrants might initially come to America *legally*, fleeing Christian persecution in their homelands. In such cases, legal immigrants might be unaware that with a nonimmigrant tourist visa, they have only one year to apply for asylum and seek resident alien status. If there are any missteps, a legal immigrant is placed in the impossible situation of having to either return to their country of persecution or remain in America, a place where they have been working and paying taxes.

Discerning Welcome blends Christian ethics and Reformed theology to embrace the political resistance of welcoming "refugees" as neighbors: "Christ's mission for Christ followers to love God and love neighbor is deeply political. When the neighbor we discover among us is a refugee, lacking legal status but seeking safety and security in our *polis*, the Christian has a *political* decision to make: whether or not to follow Christ, by welcoming the refugee into the community, as God's own creation and a neighbor in need."[17] Although *Discerning Welcome* only addresses refugees, a particular class of immigrants named by the United Nations, the overarching point is that Christians must deliberately engage in a process of theological discernment as it relates to immigration when the "laws of the land" conflict with what they ethically feel to be the "laws of God"!

The numerous instances where immigration appears in Scripture show that God uses immigration to bring people to a greater understanding of God's will for human creation. Accordingly, congregations should distinguish between laws that uplift and those that degrade humanity. This is indeed a basis for prophetic preaching directly flowing from prophetic leadership. Stated otherwise, as Martin Luther King Jr. wrote in his famous "Letter from Birmingham City Jail," quoting Saint Augustine, "an unjust law is no law at all."[18] Faith communities should provide sanctuary to those facing potential deportation, following the biblical example of welcome, by aiding immigrants in need. This is a way churches can practice *civil disobedience* as an act of *divine obedience*.

A Faith-Based Call to Action: Offering Sanctuary through Civil Disobedience

Scripture's consistent position on immigration shows it has been used as a divine tool to integrate diverse peoples. If the Bible is indeed the ultimate moral authority for Christian faith communities, the question must be raised as to whether the United States' recent immigration practices reconcile with one's faith-based morality.

When the answer has been no, history shows that persons of faith have engaged in the prophetic work of civil disobedience, a part of the resistance politics that falls squarely with the prophetic domain of ministry. Indeed, this type of religious activism, expressed through the 1980s Sanctuary Movement, was theologically like the civil disobedience King employed during the civil rights movement.

Civil Disobedience in the Sanctuary Movement

Although reignited in response to #MAGA policies and its political narrative, the debate around immigration and immigration reform, along with the associated theological conundrum, is most certainly not new.

The Sanctuary Movement began in the 1980s as a faith-based response to America's policies that made political asylum difficult for Central Americans fleeing civil conflict.[19] At the time, the Reagan administration denied refuge to Central American applicants for political asylum.[20] As early as 1981, religious leaders showed their opposition by helping Central American refugees enter the United States. Reverend John Fife of the Southside Presbyterian Church in Tucson, Arizona, declared his church to be a sanctuary for refugees in 1982. Many churches in other parts of the United States subsequently followed suit. By 1985, it is believed that more than two hundred churches were involved in the Sanctuary Movement, assisting refugees by providing them with transportation away from border states, housing, and food and helping them find employment.[21]

The term *sanctuary* was often invoked in the prophetic context to protest the federal government's practice of deporting undocumented Salvadorans. The theological basis for the Sanctuary Movement can be traced back to Levitical cities where priests were designated as arbitrators and protectors of those seeking refuge. Joining the Sanctuary Movement, therefore, was an act of civil disobedience that significantly increased in ecclesial and faith-based communities that took moral issue with governmental policies adversely affecting immigrants.

In following the example that Levitical priests set, the clergyperson has a unique role in the resistance politics of civil disobedience.[22] In other words, within the prophetic domain of leadership, "offering sanctuary to fugitives is but a continuation of a Judeo-Christian tradition."[23] As in the Old Testament, where "God's law could be invoked in opposition to civil law," many took significant issue with the Reagan administration and in turn practiced civil disobedience through the Sanctuary Movement.[24]

Civil Disobedience in the Civil Rights Movement

Almost ten years after writing *Stride toward Freedom: The Montgomery Story*, a chronicle of the Montgomery bus boycott's success and the philosophical basis for his prophetic leadership therein, while incarcerated, King responded to church leaders' refusal to allow their denominations and respective congregations to engage in secular politics. In 1963, King wrote "Letter from Birmingham City Jail," squarely addressing fellow clergypersons who criticized his activism, speaking to the need to disobey "unjust laws," while also arguing that those who acquiesce to evil participate in promoting it and are consequently agents of evil, too."[25] If one refuses to acquiesce to systemic evils—whether they be flawed immigration policies or Jim Crow laws—that refusal will manifest through civil disobedience as part of prophetic leadership.

King expounded on his discernment between "just" and "unjust" laws as a justification for civil disobedience: "A just law is a man-man code that squares with the moral law or the law of God. An unjust law is a law that is out of harmony with the moral law."[26] In living out this philosophy, it was King's prophetic resistance on Good Friday, April 12, 1963, that gave rise to his incarceration for violating an injunction and his subsequent authorship of the famed letter.

In *Walker v. City of Birmingham*, the Supreme Court records that in the days prior to King's arrest, he and other Black ministers unsuccessfully applied for a parade permit to protest the city's discriminatory conditions.[27] In denying their application, Birmingham's police commissioner, Eugene "Bull" Connor, publicly remarked, "No, you will not get a parade permit in Birmingham, Alabama to picket. I will picket you over to City Jail."[28] While incarcerated in Birmingham City Jail, King addressed the ongoing necessity for oppressed religious groups to engage in the prophetic resistance of civil disobedience.

That'll Preach!

In the African American clergy context—as an ode to Karl Barth's time-honored axiom "The preacher should preach with the Bible in one hand and the newspaper in the other"—we often say, "That'll preach!" In other words, when a practical occurrence has a biblical basis and should be widely shared as an enriching part of a faith community's journey, that occurrence is worthy of pulpit promulgation.

In considering the contemporary impact of "Letter from Birmingham City Jail," including the widely publicized 2020 #BlackLivesMatter protests—acts of morally based civil disobedience that were rooted in demands for social justice. Such protests prove that civil disobedience remains as relevant today as it was in 1963. Moreover, in considering the fact that immigration is one of the most significant social justice issues the current church is facing, the church should engage in a renewed Sanctuary Movement.

Inasmuch as the church's historical engagement in social justice movements stems from the motivation of prophetic preaching, such a movement will require more social justice–oriented pastors to prophetically preach on the practice of civil *disobedience* and the correlating importance of divine *obedience*.

Civil Disobedience and Contemporary Immigration Reform

The tension between "just" and "unjust" laws that King addressed in "Letter from Birmingham City Jail" is not new for faith communities. When Syrian refugees were fleeing to Canada in December 2015, a church sign was posted that reminded passersby this was not a new situation: "Christmas: A Story about a Middle East Family Seeking Refuge."[29] Indeed, scripture shows that Jesus too was part of a migrant family who fled persecution in their native land and sought refuge in a foreign one (Matt 2:13–15). Perhaps those who feel the church's role is not to be engaged in politics should be more empathic and (re)consider the fact that God used the one who gave us the church as a precursor to the many Latinx and Haitian nationals who seek refuge at the US border.

Further, in light of this ongoing tension and the biblically based moral imperative to resist laws that negate human worth, we must remember that under Pharaoh, the Egyptian government required that Hebrew midwives murder newborn boys (Exod 1:15–21); the Babylonian king Nebuchadnezzar required all people, regardless of their religious affiliation, to bow down before a statue of his image (Dan 3); and Roman authorities forbade the earliest apostles from proclaiming the name of Jesus (Acts 5:27–28). Moreover, there's the example of Peter and the apostles who obeyed

God's teaching—instead of human authority—when they continued to teach others about Jesus, even when such teaching was illegal (Acts 5:29). The Bible clearly calls on faith communities to a higher law when the laws of the land do not reconcile with moral authority. Pastors should remind congregations of their moral duty through the practice of prophetic preaching.

Just as King, in writing "Letter from Birmingham City Jail," highlighted the difference Saint Augustine drew between "just" and "unjust" laws, the apostle Paul drew a similar distinction in writing his letter to the Philippians. Just as Paul noted the difference between the morals of this world and citizenship in heaven (Phil 3:20), the church's prophetic leaders should embrace a theology of welcome—an immigration perspective that is consistent with both Scripture and our heavenly citizenship—and prophetically preach in a way that is consistent with this perspective. A renewed Sanctuary Movement is already underway.

Conclusion

Just as the fight for civil rights is an ongoing movement, the same can be said for immigration reform. Considering the United States' current immigration posture, faith adherents should be engaged, consistent with the call issued by Mayor Lumumba in Jackson, Mississippi.

Scripture teaches its readers to provide welcome to strangers in a foreign land. The children of Israel were once in that category, as was Jesus, Scripture's most famous immigrant refugee. As a minority living in the United States, I take to heart the country's history of welcoming immigrants. As explained in the following chapter, I am wary to embrace the proverbial melting pot for today, notwithstanding its application in yesteryear. Indeed, consistent with America's demographics, most Americans have an ancestry that places their families as strangers in a foreign land too.

THE PRACTICE OF PROPHETIC PREACHING

Prepare your work outside, get everything
ready for you in the field;
and after that, build your house.

—Proverbs 24:27

I moved from my hometown in Louisiana, where I served a congregation I knew, to serve a congregation I didn't know in North Carolina. To put my transition in terms of a sports analogy, although I didn't know the *players*, I did know the *playbook*. Because of the Methodist itineracy system of moving pastors from church to church, under the appointment of a presiding bishop—before being assigned to lead St. Joseph in North Carolina—I had already successfully coached three "teams" in Louisiana. I did so with a small congregation in a rural area (in Tangipahoa Parish), another congregation in uptown New Orleans, and another in Historic St. James, the city's oldest predominately Black Protestant church and the first congregation the AME Church established in the Deep South. My playbook consists of what I call the "practice of prophetic preaching,"

Prophetic preaching is preaching that invokes a response. It is intended to make a congregation look at larger social issues and see their connection to society at large in responding to matters of social injustice. The *practice* of prophetic preaching, therefore, involves developing a sustained sequence of events that connects the sacred *and* secular as well as the liturgical *and* political to ensure that members of the congregation have the opportunity, week after week, to see themselves as part of a Jesus-oriented solution to social problems.

My congregation at St. Joseph, in Durham, was thriving before the Covid-19 pandemic, and it continued to thrive for the remainder of 2020, the shutdown year, and throughout the shutdown periods of 2021. The preaching focused on connecting the treasures of the Holy Bible with twenty-first-century occurrences. Recall Karl Barth's famous expression "The preacher should preach with the Bible in one hand and the newspaper in the other." My practice of prophetic preaching was and remains centered on a church calendar that addresses social justice issues. The circumstances proved that God's people needed God's preachers to deliver a liberating word and congregations to act on it. To return to the question posed by Paul, "How can they hear without a preacher?" (Rom 10:14).

Social Circumstances Will Define How the Prophet Will Preach

At face value, my personal experience in leading two congregations as a prophetic preacher is counterintuitive: One of the best things that could have happened to my ministry, giving me the momentum to create excitement and draw members to the church, was the right-wing reaction to the presidency of Barack Obama. The reactionary rise of the "Make America Great Again" (#MAGA) narrative created the platform for me to draw others into the church at a time when many argue the church's influence is waning. Stated otherwise, membership increased, along with operational capacity, in two different congregations—Historic St. James in New Orleans and St. Joseph in Durham—because of our *practice* of prophetic preaching.

During CNN's election returns in November 2016, commentator Van Jones was shocked at the *backlash*, which he called *whitelash*, where white evangelicals and a conservative culture rebuked a progressive American agenda and the success of Obama's presidency by electing Donald Trump.[1] Although Trump has long left the White House, at the time of this book's final edits, in late 2022, the chorus of "Trumpetts" plays on in the continued politics and policies of the #MAGA narrative.

The #MAGA chorus created a new boogeyman of critical race theory (CRT), an academic discipline studied in graduate and professional schools that seeks to critique the role race plays in America, in responding to the slow-moving pace of the post–civil rights movement era.[2] This definition, one that I personally studied more than twenty years ago in law school, doesn't even remotely resemble the definition recently manufactured by right-wing political leaders to create fear and capitalize on an undercurrent of racialized polarization throughout the United States. Instead, the recently reintroduced *and reimaged* CRT is being used as a threat to the exceptionalism of white America and as a rallying force for conservatives. This deliberate mislabeling is a call for prophetic preaching.

The Trumpetts played their rallying song of division in 2021 when "Stop the steal" became the new mantra of opponents to the November 2020 free and fair elections, after the failed insurrection at the US Capitol on January 6. Legislatures in states like Texas and Georgia adopted new photo ID requirements, along with onerous restrictions on voting, like closing precincts in predominately African American neighborhoods while also reducing polling place hours. These voter suppression attempts and legalized barriers to citizen participation became a de facto imposition of poll taxes on poor and minority voters. Because the #MAGA chorus sings on—as a nod to the time-honored expression "When life gives you lemons, *make lemonade*"—America's current sociopolitical circumstances present ongoing opportunities for pastors to attract and engage a more progressive and justice-oriented demographic with the practice of prophetic preaching.

Those who demonstrated in the civil rights movement were largely raised in the church. Those who demonstrated in the much more recent #BlackLivesMatter movement, however, embraced an organizing that rejected "religion" while simultaneously adhering to the morality of its practice, choosing to be *spiritual* and not religious. The time is, therefore, ripe for prophetic pastors to plan church calendars that are more than just liturgical—they need to plan church calendars that are responsive to the social changes and movements surrounding them. Remember the foundational question raised in chapter 1: "When does the church get political?"

The goal of planning the church's operations around such a calendar may or may not be "evangelistic" by seeking to bring others to Christ as members of the local congregation. In my experience, the church's relevance in addressing social justice issues while being at the forefront of community leadership always draws more people to its doors and engages more people in its work.

The church gets political in response to oppressive social conditions. This cause-and-response pattern has been true throughout history, as faith leaders have taken the moral high ground in responding to social injustices the church simply could not ignore. However, the church should not just "get political." Social circumstances dictate that the church should *stay* political because it must plan to address social inequities in a deliberately sustained fashion. Prophetic preaching with a planned church calendar can create a culture of belonging for the "churched" and "unchurched" alike.

I Heard the Call for Prophetic Preaching: #SocialJusticeSunday Was Born

In May 2019, shortly after I was appointed to serve St. Joseph, I engaged in a deliberate listening session based on proven onboarding success strategies.[3] In meeting with each church auxiliary and many individual stakeholders, my announced practice was to "listen more and talk less." At the conclusion of my ninety-day listening tour, my church held the first church-wide meeting of my administration.

I needed to have complete buy-in for a paradigm shift, as I gave the congregation a PowerPoint presentation that represented their collective voice. Based on their responses, I developed a SWOT (strengths, weaknesses, opportunities, and threats) analysis and discussed potential recommendations. I consistently heard members proudly speak of St. Joseph's 150-year history that was steeped in "prophetic leadership" and "social justice" (my words). When I said "prophetic leadership," I saw some confused faces and others that looked intrigued. But when I said "social justice," almost every face lit up! I can honestly say that the mention of "Jesus" and "social justice" brought people joy and excitement. The two go hand in hand.

As part of that first meeting, we unanimously adopted a church calendar that included the scheduling of four #SocialJusticeSundays: quarterly worship services that would embrace the honored tradition of prophetic leadership, along with the politics of preaching. Indeed, the New Testament's four Gospel narratives show that Jesus set a foundation for the church's birth by opposing the oppression Jews experienced under the Roman Empire. In attempting to mirror Jesus's prophetic example, St. Joseph's first #SocialJusticeSunday was to oppose the social oppression of the #MAGA narrative being told throughout the country!

Less than two months into my pastorate, my church honored Virginia Williams, a longtime church member who was a part of Durham's Royal Ice Cream sit-in on June 23, 1957, an orchestrated act of civil disobedience that preceded both the famous February 1, 1960, lunch counter sit-ins in Greensboro, North Carolina, and the 1961 Freedom Rides, college student–coordinated rides on Trailways and Greyhound buses that tested segregation laws in interstate commerce. Our special guests included Black fraternities and social justice groups that were instrumental in supporting the Royal Seven protesters, through the leadership of William A. Marsh, Esq., a former St. Joseph member who has transitioned on but represented the protesters in court.

With a recognition of the present, my church also celebrated the social progress resulting from civil disobedience by honoring the Honorable Anita Earls, founder of the nonprofit law firm the Southern Coalition for Social Justice, who had recently been elected to serve as an associate justice of the North Carolina Supreme Court. In what I was told was a timely and relevant message, I preached a prophetic sermon that championed civil disobedience—"God Will Protect and God Will Provide"—based on the famed story of Shadrach, Meshach, and Abednego (Dan 3).

St. Joseph's second #SocialJusticeSunday was the third Sunday of August 2019, three days before the anniversary of the August 28, 1963, March on Washington. With a thematic focus of "Jobs, Justice, and Education," we welcomed Vice President Kamala Harris, then a member of the US Senate and candidate for president, along with North Carolina Supreme Court chief justice Cheri Beasley, the first African American woman to serve in that capacity. My church also welcomed the city's mayor and a host of locally elected officials, along with Vice President Harris's beloved Alpha Kappa Alpha Sorority, Inc., on its annual International Day of Prayer. With an overflow crowd size the church had never before seen, I preached another prophetic sermon, "And When Does the Church Get Political?," based on Jeremiah 8:18–22. Without being *partisan*, I was indeed most certainly *political*. I criticized several Trump administration policies by likening their irreparable damage to the United States to King Nebuchadnezzar's destruction of Jerusalem during the Babylonian exile.

Subsequent #SocialJusticeSundays have included honoring US ambassador Andrew Young as well as hosting Reverend Dr. William J. Barber II, an especially gifted prophetic preacher, in placing an emphasis on voting. St. Joseph also hosted Marc H. Morial—the longtime president and CEO of the National Urban League, one of America's preeminent civil rights organizations—for a special #SocialJusticeSunday in October 2022, as we encouraged people throughout the community to caravan with us for a #SoulsToThePolls and take advantage of early voting.

Our #SocialJusticeSundays did more than bring big crowds. They reimagined the congregation with the local community, as a body of faithful Christians who were not just concerned about salvation in the kingdom to come. Through the gift of prophetic preaching, we showed this congregation's leadership in addressing systemic injustices in the kingdom at hand.

#SocialJusticeSundays now occupy four of the fifty-two Sundays of the year. Four other Sundays are populated with #NCCUSunday, a quarterly day of philanthropy to celebrate historically Black colleges and universities (HBCUs) by raising funds for neighboring North Carolina Central University (NCCU). St. Joseph typically hosts students, along with the university's chancellor and other members of the administration, while also welcoming graduates who do not belong to the church. A great example of our success was the last Sunday of February 2022.

On February 27, 2022, as St. Joseph celebrated another #NCCUSunday, we honored the larger contribution HBCUs have made to America. This Sunday was especially noteworthy because, as it was the celebratory end to Black History Month, the month began on anything but a celebratory tone. On February 1, racist extremists called in orchestrated bomb threats to several HBCUs

around the country. In Durham, as NCCU students had to evacu-
ate their dormitories, the university's chancellor and provost led
them to St. Joseph to take refuge. By the month's end, however,
on #NCCUSunday, St. Joseph welcomed Dr. Glenda Baskin Glover,
president of Tennessee State University and international president of Alpha Kappa Alpha Sorority, Inc., along with Dr. Willis L.
Lonzer III, general president of my beloved fraternity, Alpha Phi
Alpha Fraternity, Inc. The collective efforts raised almost $100,000
in scholarship funds while also receiving news coverage on every
local network. The focus on addressing both spiritual and temporal
matters through the domain of prophetic leadership is organized
each year through the church calendar. An appropriate expression
provides, "Plan your work and work your plan." That's exactly what
we do at St. Joseph.

Other Sundays are populated by an annual Lay Day, honoring the laity's ministry, as well as the annual church anniversary
Sunday. There's even an annual day set aside as Pastor's Appreciation Sunday. Praise God! Churches can almost always expect larger
showings on Resurrection Sunday and the Sunday closest to Christmas. Those Sundays make up about thirteen Sundays. What about
the other thirty-nine? How do the pastor and church leadership
create a culture of belonging, where people don't want to miss the
excitement of church on *any* given Sunday? They do so by allowing the sacred to meet the secular with a church calendar that
embraces the practice of prophetic preaching every Sunday.

Creating a Theology of Welcome Where the Sacred Meets the Secular

One of the treasures of Methodism is its annual system that allows
church leaders to both quantitatively *and* qualitatively measure
effectiveness. Since a geographically assigned presiding bishop
makes pastoral appointments at a regularly scheduled annual

conference, the pastor and congregation each have the great opportunity to introspectively reflect on the past and simultaneously plan
for the future. Regardless of whether a denomination has an annual
conference, synod meeting, or adjudicatory gathering, I highly recommend that pastors plan an annual church calendar, with the
church universal's liturgical calendar serving as a starting point.

An additional time to begin, especially in traditions where
there is an annual gathering, is immediately after the annual meeting. It gives everyone in the congregation an opportunity to get
behind a new attempt to bring the ministry of Jesus to people in a
clear and predictable pattern. There's also something very special
about the joyful anticipation of the Advent season. The four weeks
before Christmas might be a great time to start the church's calendar too. In my case, although the liturgical calendar begins in late
November, with the first Sunday of the Advent season, St. Joseph's
church calendar begins May 1, coinciding with the new conference
year that begins immediately following the regularly scheduled
annual conference, usually in late April or the first week of May.

Before moving to Durham, when I served congregations in
New Orleans, my practice was conceptually the same. Because
the regularly scheduled annual conference was typically in mid-
October, the new conference year began on October 1. In both
scenarios, the intent is identical: the pastor has an opportunity
to prophetically (and politically) engage the community while
planning the prophet's work to go together with the liturgy of
the church.

Incorporating the Sacred and Secular
in January, February, and March

Prophetic preaching is not limited to the Bible's Prophetic Books
and is not something that's separate from typical preaching. It's
instead an informed and deliberate hermeneutical approach to
interpreting Scripture that seeks to prompt a reaction from the

congregation. In the same realm, the practice of planning a church calendar that emphasizes the church's prophetic leadership role in creating a theology of welcome should *not* be separate and apart from the church's annually recognized liturgical traditions.

When the two are brought together in the planning process, they make for rich and seasonally anticipatory ministries that excite parishioners so that they never want to miss church because something is *always* happening. Moreover, connecting the two is also an opportunity to reach those who are not members of the congregation—and may not be members of any congregation—by showing that the church's work in prophetic leadership must allow it to be a place of welcome for those who traditionally will not go to church on Sunday mornings.

To incorporate the sacred and secular as the prophetic practice of preaching, begin by considering the first two quarters of a calendar year: January through March and April through June. The two quarters bring together opportunities for worship that are celebratory, along with opportunities for cathartic lament. The respective months present opportunities to celebrate traditions of the past while simultaneously honoring social progress that is made in the present. Most importantly, however, the two quarters present the prophetically focused pastor with opportunities to incorporate deeply spiritual liturgical traditions with regularly observed social traditions that create a culture of inclusion and belonging for *all* God's children.

January, February, and March present opportunities for both celebration and deep introspective reflection, where the church can become a beacon of light for the community if planning and outreach are appropriately done. January begins in a celebratory way, with the Christmas season and the Feast of the Epiphany on January 6. As a means of enhancing or embellishing liturgical excitement, I also encourage parishioners to be sure to attend the first worship experience of the New Year, during which I typically invite everyone to receive a special blessing, along with the imposition of olive oil on their foreheads, as they recommit themselves to Christ.

On the first Sunday of January 2021 and in following the Revised Common Lectionary, I preached from the preselected gospel reading (John 1:1–18), with the assigned sermonic topic, "Begin Again," as a nod to Eddie Glaude's book by the same name. I created an atmosphere of optimism, even during a pandemic and only months after the public spectacle of George Floyd's vicious murder. Only weeks before the historic inauguration of a new administration and only days before the failed January 6 insurrection at the US Capitol, I reminded congregants that civic responsibility cannot be lost. Each time we refuse to abdicate civil responsibility and work toward the concept of democracy, we choose to "begin again."[4] That Sunday was a classic example of how prophetic preaching should combine with church traditions to make the Bible as relevant today as it was when the respective texts were originally written. By following the liturgical calendar and combining it with the practice of prophetic preaching, my first sermon of that year was both liturgically and socially relevant.

Moving from the sacred focus of what scriptures are used in worship and pivoting to the secular sphere of what's happening outside of church culture, approximately two weeks after the January 6 Feast of the Epiphany, the annual Martin Luther King Jr. Sunday presents an opportunity for a congregation to come together around a theme of diversity while welcoming others from the community who might not otherwise be a part of traditional worship. I have benefited from this practice while receiving local news coverage that highlights how the church is "living out" King's dream. Indeed, each year I deliberately plan to live out King's dream in a way that honors human diversity while creating a communal space of inclusion and belonging. Such public celebrations do much more than honor King's birth. They celebrate the principles to which he dedicated his life.

In my professional experience, even though each of the four congregations I have served as a senior pastor was drastically different, the outcome was predictably the same: our outward-facing perspective caused others in the community to recognize the congregation's emphasis on social justice, as external organizations (for-profit, nonprofit, and governmental) looked to partner with the congregation on future matters where the community's welfare could be served. In New Orleans, for example, Dillard University's Office of External Relations partnered with Historic St. James in planting community gardens and creating more "green space" in urban communities. Similarly, IberiaBank partnered with us in addressing the importance of home ownership. In Durham, after vaccines were developed to combat the Covid-19 virus, St. Joseph was invited to host several on-site vaccine clinics with the municipal government and several leading health-care providers. The congregation also received grant funds from a variety of benefactors, including Duke University, to serve food to the vulnerable homeless population.

I took away at least two things from my pastoral service in New Orleans: people love good music and really love good food. The celebration of Black History Month is a great time to share in both. In planning out the four Sundays of February, I like to reserve one Sunday celebration for Music of the Movement and another for an official Black History Month program and food festival, with invited guests. In the African American church tradition, Music of the Movement might mean the omission of a sermon and a truncated order of liturgy so the congregation can worship God by joining the freedom struggle for liberation in song. In other congregations, it might mean that the choral ministry is deliberate in learning some of the songs that have undergirded the Black existence as a way to say that others are welcome or to simply enjoy some good music!

February is also a great time to host guest preachers. As a native of New Orleans, I have unabashedly shared that gumbo is my favorite food. It is a rich diversity of ingredients that come together to make a special treat. As a pastor, I see myself as a chef who makes a "liturgical gumbo." My year-round preaching is like a roux, a gumbo's baseline substance, forming a foundation for the diversity of ingredients that go into the dish. When I invite guest preachers to share their unique preaching voices by contributing their ingredients to a special recipe, one preacher provides the shrimp. Another provides the okra. Still another provides the sausage. February is a great time, regardless of *any* congregation's demographics, to bring in guest preachers and liven up the congregation's pallet with a variety of textual interpretations that are rich and complementary to the senior pastor.

With all this talk about food, given the rich traditions of culinary excellence that come from the African American community, I also encourage an ethnic food festival after one of February's Sunday worship experiences. Since "ethnic" is obviously based on context, this might include Germanic and Asian cuisine in one congregation or Ethiopian and Thai food in another. The point is that it's a time of cultural recognition and pride that fosters both knowledge and belonging.

In my context, on the last Sunday in February 2020—only weeks before the Covid-19 pandemic changed life as we knew it—St. Joseph welcomed Reverend Dr. Mark Kelly Tyler, the senior pastor of Mother Bethel AME Church in Philadelphia (the congregation that owns the first parcel of real estate acquired by African Americans), as we wore traditional Western African attire (e.g., kente fabric), before hosting a celebration of African cuisine. The main point of February—especially in majority-white congregations—is to worship God while showing that Martin Luther King Jr. wasn't the only African American who contributed to the Black freedom struggle and also creating a culture of inclusiveness and belonging where all people feel appreciated and welcomed. Sharing an ethnic meal after worship is an opportunity to not just fellowship but both literally and figuratively sink your teeth into another culture.

March is a time when the sacred and secular literally meet. In addition to typically beginning the sacrificial liturgical season of Lent, March is also Women's History Month. We should deliberately celebrate the accomplishments women have made in society. One of the great ironies of the church is that although women compose the majority of most congregations' membership rolls while often playing active leadership roles in their respective congregations, there is often still a stigma and prejudice that frowns on women in the pulpit. Deliberately calling out and fighting against this stigma means hosting women preachers and lay speakers. On one Sunday in March 2021, during the Covid-19 pandemic, our congregation virtually heard from Kristi Jones, a powerful lay speaker who is the first woman to serve as chief of staff to a North Carolina governor in the history of the state. During the month of March, even with the sacrificial focus on Lent, St. Joseph is very deliberate in creating an affirming culture of inclusion that empowers women while focusing on their leadership and contributions to society.

Incorporating the Sacred and Secular in April, May, and June

In my professional clergy experiences, an effective church calendar will connect both the sacred and the secular. Connecting the two is not only an opportunity to preserve and celebrate the church's rich liturgical traditions but also an opportunity to create a place of welcome in establishing a culture of "belonging" to attract both individuals and groups who might be considered "unchurched." Stated otherwise, connecting the sacred and the secular in a church calendar is an opportunity to galvanize those who might be less concerned about the "kingdom to come" and only focused on the "kingdom at hand" around the good work of the church's social justice mission and prophetic activism.

The Sunday closest to April 22 is a great time for Environmental Justice Sunday because it falls closest to Earth Day—unless
this Sunday is the high holy observation of Palm Sunday or Resurrection Sunday, depending on how early the Lenten season begins.
In recent years, I have preached prophetic sermons from Revelation and Genesis, reminding worshippers of our dominion and
duty of creation care (Gen 1:26), especially considering Scripture's
representation that Jesus will return to the earth and be with us,
where the throne will be among mortals (Rev 21:2–3). Consistent
with the overarching theme of Lent, such prophetic preaching
around Earth Day is indeed a call to repent from habits that poison
the planet and pollute the earth.

Further, May is the time we celebrate Mother's Day as well
as honor graduates and those who are being promoted from one
grade to the next. What a wonderful time to have another social
event. Something as simple as a potluck meal offered to the community gives people a chance for fellowship. When I served in New
Orleans, we hosted a quarterly jazz concert with Delfeayo Marsalis
and the Uptown Jazz Orchestra each May. This spring concert was
not only a chance for additional fellowship among members of the
church but also an opportunity to draw people from the community who otherwise might never engage with a local congregation.

June marks the weeks after Easter and leading into Pentecost,
the liturgical time when the church universal celebrates Jesus's
post-resurrection appearances (the popular stories of Doubting
Thomas and the Walk to Emmaus quickly come to mind) or maybe
even the diversity of Pentecost Sunday (Acts 2). June is also a special
time of belonging, where again the sacred and secular connect in
the most celebratory ways. Stated otherwise, June is a particularly
important time for prophetic preaching!

As a way of empowering our gay brothers and sisters, the
church calendar should also recognize that June is the celebration
of Pride Month in America. In June 2019, the month after my initial

assignment to serve St. Joseph and only weeks after the congregation's first #SocialJusticeSunday, I preached on the topic "We All Have a Part to Play." Using the psalmist's words as a guide—"Let everything that breathes praise the Lord" (Ps 150:6)—through the diversity of Black and white as well as straight and gay, we created an empowering and festive space where we reclaimed church as a "safe space." In the weeks that followed, I saw an increased return of several congregants' family members who previously felt judged and castigated in the place that is supposed to show others Jesus's love.

More recently, on Pentecost Sunday in June 2022, I did the same thing. In beginning the sermon with a reference to the communal diversity of good gumbo,[5] I called out the politics of "Otherism" that castigates Blacks, immigrants, and Jews in the form of Christian nationalism while also calling out the xenophobia behind the great white replacement theory that motivated the violent shootings at Mother Emanuel AME Church in Charleston, South Carolina (2015), and the Tops grocery store in Buffalo, New York (2022), and criticizing the homophobia behind the shooting spree at Pulse, a nightclub in Orlando, Florida (2015). The gumbo metaphor in sermons is a much more inclusive version of the melting pot reference of yesteryear. Gumbo's inclusiveness speaks to a communal place of authentic welcome where there is no competition or fear of replacement. Differences complement, not compete. June is a time for prophets to preach, highlighting the mosaic nature of America!

The Easter season is a festive time when Christians celebrate Jesus's resurrection. By observing June as Pride Month at St. Joseph, we were able to resurrect hope and create a culture of belonging in a space that is all about love. Indeed, Jesus's sacrificial love for humanity should invoke a mutual love among humans that includes an appreciative and respectful love for our queer brothers and sisters too. It's about taking risks, about grafting a family together from nothing, about being tenacious in the face of ridicule—surely Jesus knew something about this kind of love.

In addition to the secular observance of Pride Month, June also presents two unique opportunities to honor Black Americans, both in lament and in celebration. As a way to call out the evil legacy of white supremacy and do the deliberate work of racial reconciliation, I highly recommend a service of lament to remember the June 17, 2015, assassination of the Emanuel Nine at Mother Emanuel AME Church in Charleston, South Carolina. In 2021, we hosted a joint evening service, welcoming Bishop Timothy M. Smith of the Evangelical Lutheran Church (the cowardly assassin's denomination) along with a multiracial and multiethnic blend of worshippers from throughout the Durham community. Revered Dr. James A. Forbes Jr., pastor emeritus of the Riverside Church of New York, preached from the same text used at the Mother Emanuel Bible study the evening of the tragedy. This occasion was deeply moving and very cathartic in bringing people toward a place of healing.

Further, on a most celebratory note, June should also include Freedom Sunday, a celebration of Juneteenth and the end of chattel slavery in the United States. More so than any other month, given the intersection of the sacred and secular, June presents the greatest opportunity to cast a wide net in attracting people to the church who otherwise might not go to any church.

Remember the Remainder of the Year: Create a Culture of Belonging in Your Context Too!

After creating a communal space of sharing during my initial listening tour at St. Joseph, I learned that Sister Gail Aiken, a beloved member of the church, had recently transitioned to glory because of sickle cell disease. The congregation wanted to honor her and her nonprofit volunteerism in Durham. We began a September observation of sickle cell disease awareness in collaboration with administrators from Duke Medical Center and other health-care providers. Even in a virtual space during the pandemic, we created a strong sense of community by asking everyone to wear burgundy, the color associated with sickle cell disease awareness, and post selfies via social media, being sure to use a hashtag for the church. That way, others would see us and know our strong sense of community too.

Similarly, with October being Breast Cancer Awareness Month, given my father's transition because of cancer and the fact that I am genetically predisposed to contract the disease, I lead the charge in wearing pink and encouraging awareness and testing for early detection. We've also had a ritualistic ceremony to pour libations and call out the names of our departed loved ones. Inevitably, because several people in the congregation were wrestling with cancer-related concerns or were still dealing with a loved one's transition, our worship became a cathartic place of emotional healing and spiritual intimacy.

October is also Domestic Violence Awareness Month. By specifically naming domestic violence as a social disorder while simultaneously calling out its prevalence and presence in some of the least expected places, we make it a point to collect donations for local shelters that serve survivors while also publicly encouraging the congregation to support the shelters on a year-round basis too. In a previous pastorate, while serving at Historic St. James in New Orleans, we engaged a local playwright and hosted a stage play, *Love Doesn't Have to Hurt*, to create a broader conversation in the community at large, partnering with social and civic organizations, to obviously raise awareness about a horrible beast. In my experience, regardless of whether attempts to raise awareness about domestic violence are publicly organized well beyond the four walls of the local congregation or whether the focus is only on creating a "safe space" for communal prayer, a consequence of developing the type of church calendar described herein is to create a culture of belonging wherein people feel deeply connected to the congregation.

This space of diversity and inclusion that leads to a culture of belonging is made possible by planning a church calendar that connects the sacredness of liturgical seasons to the secular nature of life away from the church building. More importantly, in serving four different congregations, I have followed this plan of action with great success in creating a space of connection, where both congregants and members of other faith and non-faith communities alike have developed an affinity for the congregation that engenders a very personal feeling of connection and belonging.

The examples I've shared have been focused on my context and the ways my local congregation has created a culture of belonging. What about celebrating Hispanic Heritage Month during the September to October time frame, especially given the incredible ways in which our Latinx brothers and sisters are joining Protestant churches? What about working with education groups and procuring backpacks and school supplies for children in August, during National Back to School Month? Each month of the year presents opportunities for pastors and church leaders to generate excitement and create a culture of belonging that speaks to individual and collective needs in both spiritual and temporal ways as the sacred and secular connect. Building such excitement and making the congregation relevant in the community—to both congregants and noncongregants alike—is typically driven by the social capital of relationships. In my experiences, many people are willing to be engaged. They only need to be asked.

Prophetic Preaching and
My Theology of Gumbo

While engaged in the work of racial reconciliation when I served at Historic St. James in New Orleans, a shared affection for good gumbo was the basis for a tabletop fellowship with a majority-white congregation, St. Paul's United Church of Christ, that sought commonality within diversity instead of Otherness. In full disclosure, however, gumbo for me is not just a great food. It's really an analogy for life.

Gumbo is a metaphor to represent human diversity in America. Some might argue that the American melting pot analogy of yesteryear *was* a call for diversity. In the current day, however, I find it inadequate to address the importance of calling out the xenophobia and Otherness that cause hate crimes and undergird the thinking of Christian nationalists that the American church must call to task.

The melting pot analogy speaks to a culture of assimilation, whereby diverse peoples give up something to "belong" and fit in. Conversely, as someone who has personally prepared his share of gumbo pots, I know that gumbo is not a soup. It's not a homogenous or one-to-two-ingredient substance. It's also not a blend or a puree.

When looking at a pot of gumbo, there is the individuality of shrimp as well as the individuality of okra, the individuality of chicken, and the individuality of sausage. The many diverse ingredients don't compete against one another. Instead, they complement one another. Moreover, to the point of Christian nationalism and the white supremacists who targeted and killed Blacks in both Buffalo and Charleston, the individuality of the respective ingredients is so appreciated, as adding to the whole, that sausage could never "replace" chicken, just as chicken could never replace oysters, and oysters could never replace crabmeat. The church must recognize the very real existence of Christian nationalism and call it out by emphasizing the gift of diversity to create a culture of belonging where the church can be an exemplar for society at large.

Conclusion and Final Takeaways

Each congregation is unique. My playbook for success is predicated on my belief that the sacred and secular must intersect to make the church relevant in modern times and allow the congregation to reach people who otherwise might not set foot in a church. Implementing the planning system detailed herein while responding to social circumstances that demand prophetic witness has allowed me to lead four different congregations in spiritual, numeric, and financial growth. As the old expression goes, "It's no secret what God can do. What God has done for others, God can also do for you!"

Prophetic leadership is often associated with preaching and literally speaking truth to power in publicly dismantling institutions that have marginalized and oppressed certain groups. Regrettably, the church has engaged in its share of marginalization too. Dismantling systemic structures privately is also about speaking truth to power and is part of prophetic leadership. It's about creating safe spaces where the "Other" can flourish and belong. That space of belonging, as a part of diversity and inclusion, is the beauty we know as the body of Christ.

Through the connection between leadership and prophetic preaching, *When Prophets Preach* is a calling for the American church's leaders to act. It has been said that if leaders want people to understand them, they must touch them in the head. But if they want people to follow them, they must touch them in the heart. Prophetic leaders who are prophetic preachers should be able to do both.

The United States needs the church's prophetic leadership now, just as much as it has at any point in its past. Prophetic leaders have consistently responded to injustices throughout America's history, just as the Bible shows that prophetic leaders consistently responded to injustices throughout Israel's history. The question of responding now, however, is not so much about the past. The question is whether the church's prophetic leaders will respond in the future. It's time to preach!

AFTERWORD

Graduating from Yale Divinity School fifty years ago, on my trip from New Haven back to my native South Carolina, I thought I was going into a war. The early seventies were a tense, conflicted time for the church, with lots of conflict and division in my denomination. General (er, uh, Bishop) put me on the front lines of the battle.

Somehow, by the work of some good teachers, or maybe the work of the Holy Spirit, I had gotten it into my head that it was my job as a preacher to make life in my congregation even more tense and conflicted!

I was sent to preach.

A long time later, when I became a Methodist bishop in Alabama, becoming thoroughly embedded in a mainline Protestant church, it seemed to me that many clergy under my care had allowed pastoral care and mercy ministry to subsume all other acts of ministry, particularly the ministry of truth-telling from the pulpit. "I'm a pastor, not a prophet," had become their excuse for a failure to engage in the prophetic ministry of truth.

We preachers are called by God to try to love and empathetically care for our people, yes. But we are to love them *in the name of Christ*, and there's no way to do that without telling them the truth and no way to tell the truth without risking conflict when our folk are made uncomfortable by Jesus's truth.

That's why I'm so grateful for Jay Augustine's book. Here's a stirring, insistent call by a prophetic pastor to join him in telling the truth from the pulpit. Jay claims the proud tradition of the historic church where he serves and shares some of his own experiences of doing politics from the pulpit. I agree with him that the church is already up to its steeples in politics, like it or not. Jesus Christ came not only to love us but also to challenge any principality or power that tempts us away from his reign.

Skillfully weaving in scripture (preachers, this book gave me lots of great biblical insights for addressing some of the pressing social, political questions of our day), Jay wonderfully nuances our notions of reconciliation, personal, social, civil, ecclesial. He has a knack for expanding our notions of reckoning, reconciliation, and repair, skillfully unpacking his concept of "salvific reconciliation."

America has problems in the present moment, but forgive Jay for thinking that our greatest problem is our need for somebody (a preacher) who loves God and people enough to tell them the truth in a culture of lies and deceit, of false gods and fake saviors.

Thus, I enjoyed this book and found it of immediate help and a strong prod in my own preaching. I'm sure you will too.

William H. Willimon
Duke Divinity School

ACKNOWLEDGMENTS

I have occasionally been asked, after perhaps preaching a revival or a social justice message, "Which one of your sermons is your favorite?" My response is typically something like, "My next one!" The sentiment behind that response is that all human beings should strive for what lies ahead, believing that with a foundation firmly established, the best is yet to come. That same sentiment, as expressed with respect to my preaching, applies to my writing. *When Prophets Preach* is better than my last book, and my next book will be better still.

Even though this book bears my name as its author, there are several others to whom I owe a debt of gratitude for their help and influence in writing this book too. I was honored to have my work selected for publication by Fortress Press, one of the leading publishers of theological books in the industry. In being selected to work under the brand of such a fine publishing company, I had the pleasure of directly working with two amazingly talented editors. I am thankful to have initially had the honor of working with Beth Gaede, the senior acquisitions editor who welcomed me to the Fortress Press family. Beth had a committed vision of how *When Prophets Preach* would make a difference in the life of both the academy and the church. For her expertise as a professional and the ways in which we worked together, I will always be thankful.

I am equally thankful that after *When Prophets Preach* was selected for publication and during my writing process, Beth introduced me to Bethany Dickerson, the very talented editor with whom

I had the honor of working to bring this book to completion. Bethany is both gifted and kind as well as talented and generous. I am so very thankful for our time together and proud of the work we produced. Bethany worked meticulously to help give life to the vision that was passed on to her. Again, I will always be thankful!

In addition to thanking two amazingly talented individuals from Fortress, I must also thank two other institutions, along with individuals who represented them, for helping and influencing me while writing this book. I thank my beloved congregation, St. Joseph AME Church in Durham, North Carolina, along with my beloved alma mater, Duke Divinity School.

We've done good work together at St. Joseph. This book is partially about congregational transformation as well as congregational public engagement, both of which were made possible at St. Joseph through the practice of prophetic preaching. St. Joseph's members now proudly say, "We're a social justice church." The members have always been part of a social justice church. Their passion for community and taking active stances to address systemic issues that drive inequality, in areas much larger than an individual congregation, were heightened because of the empathy and caring that have always been there. That empathy was touched and heightened through prophetic preaching.

Inasmuch as I am thankful to St. Joseph as a congregation, I am also especially thankful to several individuals who acted on its behalf. I recognize that one always runs a risk when "naming names," in that some names will be omitted. In this case, however, I am willing to take the chance. The members of St. Joseph know I love them. These names *only* speak to new ministries that were birthed between May 2019 and August 2022 through our practice of prophetic preaching. First, for the overall and unconditional support provided to me by the lay leadership, I am most thankful to serve God with Brother Reginald J. Johnson, Esq., St. Joseph's steward pro tempore; Sister Azzie Conley, St. Joseph's treasurer;

and Brother William A. "Drew" Marsh, Esq., St. Joseph's trustee pro tempore. Along with Niki Wright, our amazingly talented and committed business operations manager, we helped transform not only a congregation but also a community.

St. Joseph birthed a new Social Justice and Voter Engagement Ministry through the servant leadership of two wonderful couples: Sister Jacque Beatty Smith and her husband, Brother Richard Smith, and Sister Shereatha Baines and her husband, Dr. Tyrone Baines. We birthed Durham CARES, the local affiliate of a national mentoring project, under the servant leadership of Sister Velez Childress and Dr. Valerie Sheares Ashby, the now president of the University of Maryland, Baltimore County. We birthed the IKEMA Youth Tutorial Ministry as well as a tripartite partnership among St. Joseph, the Durham County Public School System, and Merck Durham to tutor local public schoolchildren through the leadership of Sister Willa "Tina" Sample and her husband, Brother Orlanda Sample.

St. Joseph was also blessed to birth two new and very necessary ministries that allowed its message to be shared well beyond the church's four walls. Brother Quan Williams led the charge, especially through the Covid-19 pandemic, in giving direction to the then new and obviously necessary Technology Committee. It made St. Joseph a twenty-first-century church. Moreover, in telling the story to others and attracting new members through publicity, Sister Pam Purifoy supervised a new Media Ministry that garnered repeated news coverage for St. Joseph's special events, all stemming from the practice of prophetic preaching. I am deeply thankful for the people at St. Joseph and especially thankful that, in May 2019, Bishop James Levert Davis thought enough of my leadership to give me the opportunity to serve.

Finally, with respect to St. Joseph, its associate ministers have hearts of gold. They are true blessings to both the congregation and its senior pastor. Valerie McIver, Erika Lewis, Linda Norflett,

Deborah Burroughs, Sequola "Cola" Collins, and Justice Hill are all extremely talented, especially loving, and an absolute joy. Again, I will always be thankful.

With respect to my beloved Duke University, I am a proud graduate of its divinity school and have the honor of serving as a member of the divinity school's Board of Visitors. I also have the honor of teaching classes like Christianity, Race, and the American Nation as well as engaging others as a missional consultant with the Duke Center for Reconciliation. Through educational, service, and teaching endeavors, I have been molded and made better by some of the "best of the best." They include one of the most influential and prolific writers the church has produced, my doctoral adviser, William H. Willimon, as well as the divinity school's former and current deans, Greg Jones, now president of Belmont University, and Edgardo Colon Emeric, a passionate and compassionate servant of the Most High. They are two of the most focused and visionary leaders from whom I have had the honor of learning.

I am also thankful to David Emmanuel Goatley, the then director of the Office of Black Church Studies who is now the president of Fuller Theological Seminary, and Regina Graham, a trusted friend and adviser, along with my colleagues from the Center for Reconciliation, Valerie Helbert and Nina Balmaceda. Additionally, inasmuch as *When Prophets Preach* is the second book I have written in two years, I made it a point to make some friends in the most important place: the library. I am grateful for the pleasant exchanges and constant encouragement graciously extended to me, especially by Lacey Hudspeth at the Duke Divinity School Library.

Last but most certainly not least, I thank and appreciate the sacrifices made by my family, especially my wonderful wife, Michelle. I love and appreciate you more than words can say!

NOTES

FOREWORD

1 Susannah Heschel, "Two Friends, Two Prophets." Plough Publishing House 2022. 11 January 2021, originally published 9 September 2018.

INTRODUCTION

1 Abraham J. Heschel, *The Prophets* (1962; New York: Harper Perennial Modern Classics, 2001).

2 Heschel, 3.

3 Marvin A. McMickle, *Where Have All the Prophets Gone? Reclaiming Prophetic Preaching in America* (Cleveland: Pilgrim, 2006), 2.

4 Laura Tubbs Tisdale, *Prophetic Preaching: A Pastoral Approach* (Louisville: Westminster John Knox, 2010), 3.

5 Tubbs Tisdale, 10.

6 Obery M. Hendricks Jr., *The Politics of Jesus: Rediscovering the True Revolutionary Nature of Jesus' Teachings and How They Have Been Corrupted* (New York: Three Leaves, 2006), 8.

7 Heschel, *Prophets*, 14.

8 Eric L. McDaniel, *Politics in the Pews: The Political Mobilization of Black Churches* (Ann Arbor: University of Michigan Press, 2008), 154.

9 McMickle, *Where Have All the Prophets Gone?*, 2.

10 Jean Lipman-Blumen, *Connective Leadership: Managing a Changing World* (New York: Oxford University Press, 2000).

CHAPTER 1

1 Richard Lischer, *The Preacher King: Martin Luther King, Jr. and the Word That Moved America* (New York: Oxford University Press, 1995), 56–61.

2   Mervyn A. Warren, *King Came Preaching: The Pulpit Power of Dr. Martin Luther King Jr.* (Downers Grove: InterVarsity, 2001), 117.

3   Martin Luther King Jr., *Stride toward Freedom: The Montgomery Story* (HarperCollins, 1958; Eugene: Wipf & Stock, 2001), 93.

4   Manning Marable, *How Capitalism Underdeveloped Black America: Problems in Race, Political Theory and Society* (Boston: South End, 1983), 196.

5   Hendricks, *Politics of Jesus*, 14.

6   In translating, Hendricks writes, "The Greek word signifying 'debts' in Jesus' prayer is *opheleimata*, which does not occur often in the New Testament, but when it does appear in any of its forms, it refers to debt or other legal obligations, not 'trespasses,' as the King James Version translates it." Hendricks, 65.

7   William H. Willimon, *Leading with the Sermon: Preaching as Leadership* (Minneapolis: Fortress, 2020), 10.

8   Kenyatta R. Gilbert, *Exodus Preaching: Crafting Sermons about Justice and Hope* (Nashville: Abingdon, 2018), ix.

9   Robin DiAngelo, *White Fragility: Why It's So Hard for White People to Talk about Racism* (Boston: Beacon, 2018), 17–19.

10   Andrew L. Whitehead and Samuel L. Perry, *Taking America Back for God: Christian Nationalism in the United States* (New York: Oxford University Press, 2020), x.

11   Kristin Kobes Du Mez, *Jesus and John Wayne: How White Evangelicals Corrupted a Faith and Fractured a Nation* (New York: Liveright, 2020), 4.

12   Alan I. Abramowitz, *The Great Alignment: Race, Party Transformation, and the Rise of Donald Trump* (New Haven: Yale University Press, 2018), 123.

13   Jack Jenkins, *American Prophets: The Religious Roots of Progressive Politics and the Ongoing Fight for the Soul of the Country* (New York: HarperOne, 2020), 70–71.

14   Phil Snider, introduction to *Preaching as Resistance: Voices of Hope, Justice, and Solidarity*, ed. Phil Snider (St. Louis: Chalice, 2018), 7.

15   See, generally, Richard S. Newman, *Freedom's Prophet: Bishop Richard Allen, the AME Church, and the Black Founding Fathers* (New York: New York University Press, 2008), 173–76; and Jonathan C. Augustine, "And When Does the Black Church Get Political? Responding in the Era of Trump and Making the Black Church Great Again," *Hastings Race and Poverty Law Journal* 17, no. 1 (2020): 87–132.

16   Dennis C. Dickerson, *The African Methodist Episcopal Church: A History* (New York: Cambridge University Press, 2020); see also Augustine, "And When Does the Black Church Get Political?"

17   Dennis C. Dickerson, "The Case for a Wesleyan Interpretation of A. M. E. Church History," in *African Methodism and Its Wesleyan Heritage: Reflections on AME Church History* (Nashville: AME Sunday School Union, 2009), 8.

18   C. Eric Lincoln and Lawrence H. Mamiya, *The Black Church in the African American Experience* (Durham: Duke University Press, 1994), 205.

19   Jonathan C. Augustine, "The Fiery Furnace, Civil Disobedience, and the Civil Rights Movement: A Biblical Exegesis on Daniel 3 and Letter from Birmingham Jail," *Richmond Public Interest Law Review* 21, no. 3 (2018): 243–62; see also Anthony B. Pinn, *The Black Church in the Post–Civil Rights Era* (Maryknoll: Orbis, 2002), 13.

20   Dickerson, *African Methodist Episcopal Church*, 7–8.

21   Lischer, *Preacher King*, 10–11.

22   Anthony E. Cook, "Beyond Critical Legal Studies: The Reconstructive Theology of Dr. Martin Luther King, Jr.," in *Critical Race Theory: The Key Underwritings That Formed the Movement*, ed. Kimberlé Crenshaw, Gary Peller, and Kendall Thomas (New York: New Press, 1995), 95.

23   Cook, 95.

24   Martin Luther King Jr., "Letter from Birmingham City Jail," in *A Testament of Hope: The Essential Writings and Speeches of Martin Luther King, Jr.*, ed. James M. Washington (New York: HarperOne, 1986), 293.

25   Martin Luther King Jr., "Love, Law, and Civil Disobedience," in Washington, *Testament of Hope*, 44–45.

26   Peter J. Paris, *Black Religious Leaders: Conflict in Unity* (Louisville: Westminster John Knox, 1991), 118.

27   Charles Marsh, *The Beloved Community: How Faith Shapes Social Justice, from the Civil Rights Movement to Today* (New York: Basic Books, 2005), 37–38.

28   Robert P. Jones, *White Too Long: The Legacy of White Supremacy in American Christianity* (New York: Simon & Schuster, 2020), 89–92.

29   Martin Luther King Jr., "Suffering and Faith," in Washington, *Testament of Hope*, 41.

30   John Lewis, with Michael D'Orso, *Walking with the Wind: A Memoir of the Movement* (New York: Simon & Schuster Paperbacks, 1998), 339–40.

31   McDaniel, *Politics in the Pews*, 5.

32   McDaniel, 98–99.

33   McDaniel, 129.

34   Paul A. Djupe and Christopher P. Gilbert, *The Prophetic Pulpit: Clergy, Churches and Communities in American Politics* (Lanham: Rowan & Littlefield, 2003), 43.

35   Jenkins, *American Prophets*, 55.

36   Lischer, *Preacher King*, 83.

37   Jenkins, *American Prophets*, 96.

CHAPTER 2

1   Elaine Aradillas and Wendy Grossman Kantor, "Racial Justice Activists on What's Next after Derek Chauvin's Conviction for George Floyd's Murder," *People*, April 21, 2021, https://people.com/crime/derek-chauvin-guilty-verdict-murdering-george-floyd-activists-next-steps.

2   Jonathan C. Augustine, *Called to Reconciliation: How the Church Can Model Justice, Diversity, and Inclusion* (Grand Rapids: Baker Academic, 2022), 56 (internal citations omitted).

3   See, generally, City of Durham, North Carolina, *Report of the Durham Racial Equity Task Force: An Urgent and Loving Call to Action*, July 22, 2020, https://www.durhamnc.gov/DocumentCenter/View/32853/FINAL-REPORT-Durham-Racial-Equity-Task-Force-72220.

4   William A. Darity Jr. and A. Kirsten Mullen, *From Here to Equality: Reparations for Black Americans in the Twenty-First Century* (Chapel Hill: University of North Carolina Press, 2020).

5   Darity and Mullen, 1–2.

6   "Read Martin Luther King Jr.'s 'I Have a Dream' Speech in Its Entirety," NPR, January 14, 2022, https://www.npr.org/2010/01/18/122701268/i-have-a-dream-speech-in-its-entirety.

7   Although the ongoing imprint of white supremacy is vast, because the concept of reparations is so very complex, I have deliberately limited this chapter on *racial reconciliation* to the reparations dialogue as it relates to African Americans. My intent is certainly *not* to minimize the harm white supremacy has done to Native peoples or Japanese Americans. At least, in their contexts, the federal government recognizes certain tribal sovereignties and paid reparations to

Native peoples as well as to Japanese Americans. With respect to African Americans, however, the debt has yet to be paid.

8   P. R. Lockhart, "Georgetown University Plans to Raise $400,000 a Year for Reparations," *Vox*, October 31, 2019, https://www.vox.com/ identities/2019/10/31/20940665/georgetown-reparations-fund -slavery-history-colleges; see also Olivia Anderson, "Virginia Theological Seminary Pays Reparations," *Alexandria Times*, June 10, 2021, https://alextimes.com/2021/06/virginia-theological-seminary-pays -reparations.

9   Darity and Mullen, *From Here to Equality*, 9 (internal citations omitted).

10   Carol Anderson, *White Rage: The Unspoken Truth of Our Racial Divide* (New York: Bloomsbury, 2017), 15–16.

11   Duke L. Kwon and Gregory Thompson, *Reparations: A Christian Call for Repentance and Repair* (Grand Rapids: Brazos, 2021), 101.

12   Spencer Perkins and Chris Rice, *More Than Equals: Racial Healing for the Sake of the Gospel*, rev. and expanded ed. (Downers Grove: InterVarsity, 2000), 17–19.

13   "Resources for Racial Reconciliation and Justice," Episcopal Church, accessed October 22, 2021, https://www.episcopalchurch.org/ ministries/racial-reconciliation/resources.

14   W. E. B. Du Bois, *The Souls of Black Folk* (1903; Las Vegas: Class American, 1999), 1.

15   Isabel Wilkerson, *Caste: The Origins of Our Discontents* (New York: Random House, 2020), 18.

16   North Carolina State Conference of the NAACP v. McCrory, 831 F.3d 204, 214 (4th Cir. 2016).

17   DiAngelo, *White Fragility*, 15–18.

18   Jennifer Harvey, *Dear White Christians: For Those Still Longing for Racial Reconciliation*, 2nd. ed. (Grand Rapids: Eerdmans, 2020), 44.

19   DiAngelo, *White Fragility*, 15–18.

20   Eddie S. Glaude Jr., *Democracy in Black: How Race Still Enslaves the American Soul* (New York: Broadway Books, 2016), 30.

21   Glaude, 59 (internal citations omitted).

22   Brenda Salter McNeil, *Roadmap to Reconciliation 2.0: Moving Communities into Unity, Wholeness and Justice* (Downers Grove: InterVarsity, 2020), 24.

23   Emmanuel Katongole and Chris Rice, *Reconciling All Things: A Christian Vision for Justice, Peace and Healing* (Downers Grove: IVP, 2008), 18.

24   Augustine, *Called to Reconciliation*, 19.

25   Augustine, 21.

26   Augustine, 45.

27   McNeil, *Roadmap to Reconciliation 2.0*, 26.

28   Desmond Tutu, *No Future without Forgiveness* (New York: Doubleday, 1997), 10.

29   Anthony B. Thompson, *Called to Forgive* (Minneapolis: Bethany House, 2019), 44.

30   See, e.g., William J. Barber II, *The Third Reconstruction: How a Moral Movement Is Overcoming the Politics of Division and Fear* (Boston: Beacon, 2016), 60.

CHAPTER 3

1   Michael W. Andrews, *The Influential Christian: Learning to Lead from the Heart* (Lanham: Rowan & Littlefield, 2021), 17.

2   Martin Luther King Jr., "Letter from Birmingham City Jail," in Washington, *Testament of Hope*, 294.

3   Dietrich Bonhoeffer, *The Cost of Discipleship* (1937; New York: Touchstone, 1995), 215.

4   DiAngelo, *White Fragility*, 17.

5   DiAngelo, 17.

6   DiAngelo, 17.

7   Glaude, *Democracy in Black*.

8   Anthea Butler, *White Evangelical Racism: The Politics of Morality in America* (Chapel Hill: University of North Carolina Press, 2021), 24.

9   Jones, *White Too Long*, 90–91.

10   Reggie L. Williams, *Bonhoeffer's Black Jesus: Harlem Renaissance Theology and an Ethic of Resistance* (Waco: Baylor University Press, 2014), 25.

11   Eric Metaxas, *Bonhoeffer: Pastor, Martyr, Prophet, Spy* (Nashville: Nelson, 2010), 108 (emphasis added).

12   Bonhoeffer, *Cost of Discipleship*, 45.

13   J. Deotis Roberts, *Bonhoeffer and King: Speaking Truth to Power* (Louisville: Westminster John Knox, 2005), 21.

14   Williams, *Bonhoeffer's Black Jesus*, 5.

15   Williams, 112.

16   Metaxas, *Bonhoeffer*, 317.

17   Roberts, *Bonhoeffer and King*, 108 (internal citations omitted).

CHAPTER 4

1   At the time of this writing, current federal law *does not* make it illegal for congregations to provide ministry-related assistance to immigrants, whether they be documented or undocumented: "With the exception of employing someone who is undocumented and not authorized to work, (which is quite clearly unlawful) none of the ways that a church as an institution . . . would interact with undocumented immigrants—welcoming them into a local church, offering English classes, running a food pantry or clothing closet, teaching them in Sunday school, or allowing them to teach Sunday school (so long as it is not a paid position)—is against the law. There is no legal requirement or expectation that a citizen report someone they suspect might not be lawfully present in this country." Matthew Soerens and Jenny Yang, *Welcoming the Stranger: Justice, Compassion, and Truth in the Immigration Debate*, rev. and expanded ed. (Downers Grove: IVP, 2018), 96.

2   O. Wesley Allen Jr., *Preaching in the Era of Trump* (St. Louis: Chalice, 2017), 25.

3   Glenn H. Utter, *Mainline Christians and U.S. Public Policy: Contemporary World Issues* (Santa Barbara: ABC-CLIO, 2007), 56.

4   Utter, 55.

5   Soerens and Yang, *Welcoming the Stranger*, 23 (internal citations omitted).

6   Alline Barros, "Five Years Later, Work of Reuniting Families Separated at US-Mexico Border Remains Unfinished," VOA, June 11, 2022, https://www.voanews.com/a/five-years-later-work-of-reuniting -families-separated-at-us-mexico-border-remains-unfinished/ 6610677.html.

7   Soerens and Yang, *Welcoming the Stranger*, 88.

8   Whitehead and Perry, *Taking America Back*, 92–93.

9   Mike Slaughter and Charles E. Gutenson, *Hijacked: Responding to the Partisan Church Divide* (Nashville: Abingdon, 2012), 17.

10   Du Mez, *Jesus and John Wayne*, 4.

11   Du Mez, 4.

12   Justin Victory, "'Dehumanizing': Jackson Mayor Slams ICE Raids, Asks Churches to Become Safe Havens," *Mississippi Clarion Ledger*, August 7, 2019, https://www.clarionledger.com/story/news/politics/ 2019/08/07/immigration-raids-jackson-mayor-calls-church-leaders -shelter-immigrants/1946239001.

13   See, generally, "AG Sessions Threatens 'Sanctuary Cities,' Mayors Fight Back," NBC News and the Associated Press, March 27, 2017, https://www.nbcnews.com/news/us-news/ag-sessions-threatens -sanctuary-cities-mayors-fight-back-n739171.

14   Tessa Berenson, "Here Are the White House's Latest Demands to End the Shutdown," *Time*, January 7, 2019, https://time.com/ 5496179/mike-pence-donald-trump-border-wall-proposal-shutdown -democrats: "The White House is holding form in its request for $5.7 billion for a border wall to end the shutdown, while also demanding billions of dollars more to address other priorities at the southern border, according to a proposal it gave Congressional Democrats."

15   Stephan Bauman, Matthew Soerens, and Issam Smeir, *Seeking Refuge: On the Shores of the Global Refugee Crisis* (Chicago: Moody, 2016), 29 (internal citations omitted).

16   Ellen Clark Clémot, *Discerning Welcome: A Reformed Faith Approach to Refugees* (Eugene: Cascade, 2022).

17   Clémot, xxi.

18   Martin Luther King Jr., "Letter from Birmingham Jail," in *The Autobiography of Martin Luther King, Jr.*, ed. Clayborne Carson (New York: Grand Central, 1998), 193.

19   See, generally, Judith McDaniel, "The Sanctuary Movement, Then and Now," *Religion & Politics*, February 21, 2017, https://religionandpolitics .org/2017/02/21/the-sanctuary-movement-then-and-now.

20   James W. Nickel, "Sanctuary, Asylum and Civil Disobedience," *In Defense of the Alien* 8 (1985): 176, https://www.jstor.org/stable/23141216.

21   Nickel.

22   Richard H. Feen, "Church Sanctuary: Historical Roots and Contemporary Practice," *In Defense of the Alien* 7 (1984): 133–35. https://www .jstor.org/stable/23141145.

23   Feen, 132.

24   Feen, 132.

25   Paris, *Black Religious Leaders*, 120–21.

26   King, "Letter from Birmingham Jail," 193.

27   Walker v. City of Birmingham, 388 U.S. 307, 307 (1967).

28   *Walker*, 388 U.S. at 325.

29   Bauman, Soerens, and Smeir, *Seeking Refuge*, 31 (internal citations omitted).

CHAPTER 5

1   Josiah Ryan, "'This Was a Whitelash': Van Jones' Take on Election Results," CNN, November 9, 2016, https://www.cnn.com/2016/11/09/politics/van-jones-results-disappointment-cnntv/index.html.

2   See, e.g., Richard Delgado, introduction to *Critical Race Theory: The Cutting Edge* (Philadelphia: Temple University Press, 1985), xviii.

3   Michael S. Watkins, *The First 90 Days: Critical Success Strategies for New Leaders at All Levels* (Boston: Harvard Business School Press, 2003).

4   Eddie S. Glaude Jr., *Begin Again: James Baldwin's America and Its Urgent Lessons for Our Own* (New York: Crown, 2020), xxiv.

5   Augustine, *Called to Reconciliation*, 1, 6–7.

BIBLIOGRAPHY

INTRODUCTION

Hendricks, Obery M., Jr. (2006). *The Politics of Jesus: Rediscovering the True Revolutionary Nature of Jesus' Teachings and How They Have Been Corrupted.* New York: Three Leaves.

Heschel, Abraham J. (1962) 2001. *The Prophets.* Reprint, New York: Harper Perennial Modern Classics.

Lipman-Blumen, Jean. (2000). *Connective Leadership: Managing a Changing World.* New York: Oxford University Press.

McDaniel, Eric L. (2008). *Politics in the Pews: The Political Mobilization of Black Churches.* Ann Arbor: University of Michigan Press.

McMickle, Marvin A. (2006). *Where Have All the Prophets Gone? Reclaiming Prophetic Preaching in America.* Cleveland: Pilgrim.

Tisdale, Laura Tubbs. (2010). *Prophetic Preaching: A Pastoral Approach.* Louisville: Westminster John Knox.

CHAPTER 1

Abramowitz, Alan I. (2018). *The Great Alignment: Race, Party Transformation, and the Rise of Donald Trump.* New Haven: Yale University Press.

Augustine, Jonathan C. (2020). "And When Does the Black Church Get Political? Responding in the Era of Trump and Making the Black Church Great Again." *Hastings Race and Poverty Law Journal* 17 (1): 87–132.

———. (2018). "The Fiery Furnace, Civil Disobedience, and the Civil Rights Movement: A Biblical Exegesis on Daniel 3 and Letter from Birmingham Jail." *Richmond Public Interest Law Review* 21 (3): 248–262.

Cook, Anthony E. (1995). "Beyond Critical Legal Studies: The Reconstructive Theology of Dr. Martin Luther King, Jr." In *Critical Race Theory: The Key Underwritings That Formed the Movement,* edited by Kimberlé Crenshaw, Neil Gotanda, Gary Peller, and Kendall Thomas, 85–102. New York: New Press.

DiAngelo, Robin. (2018). *White Fragility: Why It's So Hard for White People to Talk about Racism*. Boston: Beacon.

Dickerson, Dennis C. (2020). *The African Methodist Episcopal Church: A History*. New York: Cambridge University Press.

———. (2009). "The Case for a Wesleyan Interpretation of A. M. E. Church History." In *African Methodism and Its Wesleyan Heritage: Reflections on AME Church History*, 8–12. Nashville: AME Sunday School Union.

Djupe, Paul A., and Christopher P. Gilbert. (2003). *The Prophetic Pulpit: Clergy, Churches and Communities in American Politics*. Lanham: Rowan & Littlefield.

Du Mez, Kristin Kobes. (2020). *Jesus and John Wayne: How White Evangelicals Corrupted a Faith and Fractured a Nation*. New York: Liveright.

Gilbert, Kenyatta R. (2018). *Exodus Preaching: Crafting Sermons about Justice and Hope*. Nashville: Abingdon.

Hendricks, Obery M., Jr. (2006). *The Politics of Jesus: Rediscovering the True Revolutionary Nature of Jesus' Teachings and How They Have Been Corrupted*. New York: Three Leaves.

Jenkins, Jack. (2020). *American Prophets: The Religious Roots of Progressive Politics and the Ongoing Fight for the Soul of the Country*. New York: HarperOne.

Jones, Robert P. (2020). *White Too Long: The Legacy of White Supremacy in American Christianity*. New York: Simon & Schuster.

King, Martin Luther, Jr. (1986). "Letter from Birmingham City Jail." In *A Testament of Hope: The Essential Writings and Speeches of Martin Luther King, Jr.*, edited by James M. Washington, 289–302. New York: HarperOne.

———. (1986). "Love, Law, and Civil Disobedience." In Washington, *Testament of Hope*, 43–53.

———. (1958) 2001. *Stride toward Freedom: The Montgomery Story*. HarperCollins. Reprint, Eugene: Wipf & Stock.

———. (1986). "Suffering and Faith." In Washington, *Testament of Hope*, 41–42.

Lewis, John (with Michael D'Orso). (1998). *Walking with the Wind: A Memoir of the Movement*. New York: Simon & Schuster.

Lincoln, C. Eric, and Lawrence H. Mamiya. (1994). *The Black Church in the African American Experience*. Durham: Duke University Press.

Lischer, Richard. (1995). *The Preacher King: Martin Luther King, Jr. and the Word That Moved America*. New York: Oxford University Press.

Marable, Manning. (1983). *How Capitalism Underdeveloped Black America: Problems in Race, Political Theory and Society*. Boston: South End.

Marsh, Charles. (2005). *The Beloved Community: How Faith Shapes Social Justice, from the Civil Rights Movement to Today*. New York: Basic Books.

McDaniel, Eric L. (2008). *Politics in the Pews: The Political Mobilization of Black Churches*. Ann Arbor: University of Michigan Press.

Newman, Richard S. (2008). *Freedom's Prophet: Bishop Richard Allen, the AME Church, and the Black Founding Fathers*. New York: New York University Press.

Paris, Peter J. (1991). *Black Religious Leaders: Conflict in Unity*. Louisville: Westminster John Knox.

Pinn, Anthony B. (2002). *The Black Church in the Post–Civil Rights Era*. Maryknoll: Orbis.

Snider, Phil, ed. (2018). *Preaching as Resistance: Voices of Hope, Justice, and Solidarity*. St. Louis: Chalice.

Warren, Mervyn A. (2001). *King Came Preaching: The Pulpit Power of Dr. Martin Luther King Jr*. Downers Grove: InterVarsity.

Whitehead, Andrew L., and Samuel L. Perry. (2020). *Taking America Back for God: Christian Nationalism in the United States*. New York: Oxford University Press.

Willimon, William H. (2020). *Leading with the Sermon: Preaching as Leadership*. Minneapolis: Fortress.

CHAPTER 2

Anderson, Carol. (2017). *White Rage: The Unspoken Truth of Our Racial Divide*. New York: Bloomsbury.

Anderson, Olivia. (2021). "Virginia Theological Seminary Pays Reparations." *Alexandria Times*, June 10, 2021. https://alextimes.com/2021/06/virginia-theological-seminary-pays-reparations.

Aradillas, Elaine, and Wendy Grossman Kantor. (2021). "Racial Justice Activists on What's Next after Derek Chauvin's Conviction for George Floyd's Murder." *People*, April 21, 2021. https://people.com/crime/derek-chauvin-guilty-verdict-murdering-george-floyd-activists-next-steps.

Augustine, Jonathan C. (2022). *Called to Reconciliation: How the Church Can Model Justice, Diversity, and Inclusion.* Grand Rapids: Baker Academic.

Barber, William J., II. (2016). *The Third Reconstruction: How a Moral Movement Is Overcoming the Politics of Division and Fear.* Boston: Beacon.

City of Durham, North Carolina. (2020). *Report of the Durham Racial Equity Task Force: An Urgent and Loving Call to Action.* July 22, 2020. https://www.durhamnc.gov/DocumentCenter/View/32853/FINAL-REPORT-Durham-Racial-Equity-Task-Force-72220.

Darity, William A., Jr., and A. Kirsten Mullen. (2020). *From Here to Equality: Reparations for Black Americans in the Twenty-First Century.* Chapel Hill: University of North Carolina Press.

DiAngelo, Robin. (2018). *White Fragility: Why It's So Hard for White People to Talk about Racism.* Boston: Beacon.

Du Bois, W. E. B. (1903) 1999. *The Souls of Black Folk.* Reprint, Las Vegas: Class American.

Episcopal Church. (n.d.). "Resources for Racial Reconciliation and Justice." Accessed October 22, 2021. https://www.episcopalchurch.org/wp-content/uploads/sites/2/2021/02/resources_for_racial_reconciliation_and_justice.pdf.

Glaude, Eddie S., Jr. (2016). *Democracy in Black: How Race Still Enslaves the American Soul.* New York: Broadway Books.

Harvey, Jennifer. (2020). *Dear White Christians: For Those Still Longing for Racial Reconciliation.* 2nd ed. Grand Rapids: Eerdmans.

Katongole, Emmanuel, and Chris Rice. (2008). *Reconciling All Things: A Christian Vision for Justice, Peace and Healing.* Downers Grove: IVP.

Kwon, Duke L., and Gregory Thompson. (2021). *Reparations: A Christian Call for Repentance and Repair.* Grand Rapids: Brazos.

Lockhart, P. R. (2019). "Georgetown University Plans to Raise $400,000 a Year for Reparations." *Vox,* October 31, 2019. https://www.vox.com/identities/2019/10/31/20940665/georgetown-reparations-fund-slavery-history-colleges.

McNeil, Brenda Salter. (2020). *Roadmap to Reconciliation 2.0: Moving Communities into Unity, Wholeness and Justice.* Downers Grove: InterVarsity.

North Carolina State Conference of the NAACP v. McCrory, 831 F.3d 204 (4th Cir. 2016).

NPR. (2022). "Read Martin Luther King Jr.'s 'I Have a Dream' Speech in Its Entirety." January 14, 2022. https://www.npr.org/2010/01/18/122701268/i-have-a-dream-speech-in-its-entirety.

Perkins, Spencer, and Chris Rice. (2000). *More Than Equals: Racial Healing for the Sake of the Gospel*. Downers Grove: InterVarsity.

Thompson, Anthony B. (2019). *Called to Forgive*. Minneapolis: Bethany House.

Tutu, Desmond. (1997). *No Future without Forgiveness*. New York: Doubleday.

Wilkerson, Isabel. (2020). *Caste: The Origins of Our Discontents*. New York: Random House.

CHAPTER 3

Andrews, Michael W. (2021). *The Influential Christian: Learning to Lead from the Heart*. Lanham: Rowan & Littlefield.

Bonhoeffer, Dietrich. (1937) 1995. *The Cost of Discipleship*. Reprint, New York: Touchstone.

Butler, Anthea. (2021). *White Evangelical Racism: The Politics of Morality in America*. Chapel Hill: University of North Carolina Press.

DiAngelo, Robin. (2018). *White Fragility: Why It's So Hard for White People to Talk about Racism*. Boston: Beacon.

Glaude, Eddie S., Jr. (2016). *Democracy in Black: How Race Still Enslaves the American Soul*. New York: Broadway Books.

Jones, Robert P. (2020). *White Too Long: The Legacy of White Supremacy in American Christianity*. New York: Simon & Schuster.

King, Martin Luther, Jr. (1986). "Letter from Birmingham City Jail." In *A Testament of Hope: The Essential Writings and Speeches of Martin Luther King, Jr.*, edited by James M. Washington. New York: HarperOne.

Metaxas, Eric. (2010). *Bonhoeffer: Pastor, Martyr, Prophet, Spy*. Nashville: Nelson.

Roberts, J. Deotis. (2005). *Bonhoeffer and King: Speaking Truth to Power*. Louisville: Westminster John Knox.

Williams, Reggie L. (2014). *Bonhoeffer's Black Jesus: Harlem Renaissance Theology and an Ethic of Resistance*. Waco: Baylor University Press.

CHAPTER 4

Allen, O. Wesley, Jr. (2017). *Preaching in the Era of Trump*. St. Louis: Chalice.

Barros, Alline. (2022). "Five Years Later, Work of Reuniting Families Separated at US-Mexico Border Remains Unfinished." VOA, June 11, 2022. https://www.voanews.com/a/five-years-later-work-of-reuniting

-families-separated-at-us-mexico-border-remains-unfinished/
6610677.html.

Bauman, Stephan, Matthew Soerens, and Issam Smeir. (2016). *Seeking Refuge: On the Shores of the Global Refugee Crisis.* Chicago: Moody.

Berenson, Tessa. (2019). "Here Are the White House's Latest Demands to End the Shutdown." *Time,* January 7, 2019. https://time.com/5496179/mike-pence-donald-trump-border-wall-proposal-shutdown-democrats.

Clémot, Ellen Clark. (2022). *Discerning Welcome: A Reformed Faith Approach to Refugees.* Eugene: Cascade.

Du Mez, Kristin Kobes. (2020). *Jesus and John Wayne: How White Evangelicals Corrupted a Faith and Fractured a Nation.* New York: Liveright.

Feen, Richard H. "Church Sanctuary: Historical Roots and Contemporary Practice." *In Defense of the Alien* 7:132–139. https://www.jstor.org/stable/23141145.

King, Martin Luther, Jr. (1998). "Letter from Birmingham Jail." In *The Autobiography of Martin Luther King, Jr.*, edited by Clayborne Carson, 187–204. New York: Grand Central.

McDaniel, Judith. (2017). "The Sanctuary Movement, Then and Now." *Religion & Politics,* February 21, 2017. https://religionandpolitics.org/2017/02/21/the-sanctuary-movement-then-and-now.

NBC News and the Associated Press. (2017). "AG Sessions Threatens 'Sanctuary Cities,' Mayors Fight Back." March 27, 2017. https://www.nbcnews.com/news/us-news/ag-sessions-threatens-sanctuary-cities-mayors-fight-back-n739171.

Nickel, James W. (1985). "Sanctuary, Asylum and Civil Disobedience." *In Defense of the Alien* 8:176–187. https://www.jstor.org/stable/23141216.

Paris, Peter J. (1991). *Black Religious Leaders: Conflict in Unity.* Louisville: Westminster John Knox.

Slaughter, Mike, and Charles E. Gutenson. (2012). *Hijacked: Responding to the Partisan Church Divide.* Nashville: Abingdon.

Soerens, Matthew, and Jenny Yang. (2018). *Welcoming the Stranger: Justice, Compassion, and Truth in the Immigration Debate.* Rev. and expanded ed. Downers Grove: IVP.

Utter, Glenn H. (2007). *Mainline Christians and U.S. Public Policy: Contemporary World Issues.* Santa Barbara: ABC-CLIO.

Victory, Justin. (2019). "'Dehumanizing': Jackson Mayor Slams ICE Raids, Asks Churches to Become Safe Havens." *Mississippi Clarion Ledger,*

August 7, 2019. https://www.clarionledger.com/story/news/politics/
2019/08/07/immigration-raids-jackson-mayor-calls-church-leaders
-shelter-immigrants/1946239001.

Walker v. City of Birmingham, 388 U.S. 307 (1967).

Whitehead, Andrew L., and Samuel L. Perry. (2020). *Taking America Back
for God: Christian Nationalism in the United States*. New York: Oxford
University Press.

CHAPTER 5

Augustine, Jonathan C. (2022). *Called to Reconciliation: How the Church Can
Model Justice, Diversity, and Inclusion*. Grand Rapids: Baker Academic.

Delgado, Richard. (1985). Introduction to *Critical Race Theory: The Cutting
Edge*. Philadelphia: Temple University Press.

Glaude, Eddie S., Jr. (2020). *Begin Again: James Baldwin's America and Its
Urgent Lessons for Our Own*. New York: Crown.

Ryan, Josiah. (2016). "'This Was a Whitelash': Van Jones' Take on Election
Results." CNN, November 9, 2016. https://www.cnn.com/2016/11/09/
politics/van-jones-results-disappointment-cnntv.

Watkins, Michael S. (2003). *The First 90 Days: Critical Success Strategies for
New Leaders at All Levels*. Boston: Harvard Business School Press.

INDEX